PATERSON PIMP PART 2

My SOUL Is Still PIMPIN'

RANDY JACKSON a.k.a JASHON

Copyright © 2010 by Randy Jackson aka Jashon

All rights reserved. No part of this book may be used or reproduced or transmitted in any form or by any means, electronic or mechanical including photocopying, recording, or by any information storage or retrieval system without express written permission from the publisher. For more information address the publisher.

Author's Note: This is a nonfiction story. It contains no fictional or composite characters. All incidents and stories are true; however some names have been changed.

Printed in the United States of America
10 9 8 7 6 5 4 3 2 1

ISBN: 978-0-578-05001-0

MY SOUL Is STILL PIMPIN'

First paperback edition

Cover Photo by: Ricky Chandler aka "Picture Man"

E-mail: Jashon763@aol.com
Website: www.ThePatersonPimp.com

Other books by Randy Jackson aka Jashon:

The PATERSON PIMP

J&M Production Publishing
507 Broadway
P.O. Box 133
Paterson, New Jersey 07514

*Contributing writers: Anthony J. Huskey, Supreme Divine Allah, She, Frederick Stone are merely included in this book for exposure purposes only. I like to help my fellow aspiring writers.

This book is dedicated to my mom:

Minnie Pearl Buie Jackson

After my first book there was so much controversy on my feelings toward my mother. My dislike as a child for her religion is one thing, but my love for her then and now is everlasting. And to even think anything less than that would be the furthest thing from the truth. She is a unique woman and I'll always admire and adore and respect her beliefs and courage.

I'll always love you mom from your youngest son and author

—Randy "Jashon" Jackson a.k.a *The Paterson Pimp.*

DEDICATION

Gerald Lamont "Merciful Allah" Robertson,
His name says it all "Merciful Allah".

Larry "Islam" Manning,
You could ask 100 people and they would all say the same thing. "Islam was kool people."

Mildred Parker (cousin),
Always nice and kind every time I saw her.

Miss Vernell Steward,
She was always so nice to me even when her niece and me were having our ups and downs. And I'll never forget the way she pronounced my name.

Sylvia D. Taylor,
You were so nice to me when I worked with you on my first real job. And I know you're looking down at us smiling.

Pershing "Modean" Wise (17th Ave),
If you didn't know "Modean" after you talked to him you would never 4 get him.

Leon "Sly" Houston (17th Ave),
Always so kool and laid back. His name "Sly" fit him so well.

Debra Hall,
A special person that I shared many smiles and much laughter with, you were the original "China Doll" and I could never forget you or your sisters: Lena, Leeann, Sabrina or the Hall family.

Zwwiyya Moore,
You always kept me laughing. You'll be deeply missed by Playboy, Baby-Doll and myself.

Bozo and Gladys Spencer,
My father and mother-in-law, who let me date and marry their daughter when I was so young and wild. Rest in Peace.

Cerese Clyburn,
Our families were and always will be close. If I could have had another big sister it would have been you.

ACKNOWLEDGMENTS

I would like to thank my photographer Ricky Chandler "Picture Man" who took the pictures for both of my book covers. His number is 862-324-5497.

I would like to thank Toni and Sergio for designing my book cover.

I would also like to thank my very, very, very close and dear friend Leatravelle Fleming Pinchom. She stood by me and gave me so much support and inspiration while I worked on my second book.

Karla Denise Baker, who I would like to give a very big thank you to. She helped me in such a big way with her knowledge in the book world. She has also taught me that you never know where your blessing will come from. She has written several books of her own under: *The Write Message: Anonymous, Spittin' 'Em Out Like BABIES, Sleepin' Wit' the Virus, Does God Have Toys in Heaven, Barracuda Bytch, Toys in the ATTIC,* and *I Cried B'tween My Legs.*

I would like to thank "WHIZ" at Tattoo Design: 862-224-3563.

Life
+
Relationships

The pain I feel won't allow me to sleep
so I have to make this poem weep,
thinking back to the joy you brought when I saw your face,
I knew I wanted to lock this feeling up inside a special place.

Every second, every minute, every month and year
I had our love locked in my heart and kept it near,
Back then, when I held you, you were everything to me,
When you were in my arms, my soul felt free.

Then, one morning, I woke up and things seemed strange
Suddenly your face and voice brought a sudden pain,
And one hour with you no longer brought 60 minutes of fun,
I could now count 60 minutes of hate one by one,
Where was the love that was felt beneath?

Beneath the way you lie, nag, and sometimes even cheat
Am I just dreaming?
Because I don't like how it feels or maybe because it's my life
through a daydream, but also real,
How much more pain can I put on paper with this pen,
Before people start to know what my feelings are within,
Well, all I can say is an ocean is so beautiful.
When the waves flow calm,
And then out of nowhere they grow big and hit like bombs.

Should we hate the ocean?
Should we hate the waves?
Should we gain fear of it and become like slaves,
Think about this poem...

When you think about life.
Because you can stand tall and put up a great fight
But just like waves in an ocean your life flows on,
But if you grow tired and give up,
Then you're dead and gone.

—Randy "Jashon" Jackson

A MESSAGE

Every tear has a story. Every smile has a reason. Situations call for decisions. Decisions that can cost pain that can cost joy—decisions that can follow us through our whole life. I once heard someone say, "God may not come when you call Him, but He's always on time."

I always kept faith in God, but confidence in myself. And as I take you down this long journey with my second book, I'll reveal my deepest secrets and life experiences. Everyone has a story to tell. You have to free your soul and your mind will follow. I have freed my soul, but my mind still leads the way.

Everyone sees me as a pimp. But I don't want to be remembered like that. People think that what they do is what they are. But that's because they don't know God.

CHAPTER 1

The PRESENT

3:45 A.M. Time to lay all my cards on the table. Here I was sitting up in a chair trying to understand where I went wrong.

I had just picked up Baby-Doll from work at the DOLL HOUSE GO-GO BAR in Irvington, New Jersey. I was in an evil and dangerous mood despite the pile of money I had sitting on my dresser. Half she had made and half I had hustled for myself. Then the BITCH questioned me about something that had happened 24 hours ago and I went ballistic. I ripped her for all the things I knew and had allowed to happen in the last 5 years. She was only dancing on the weekends. She had gained almost 50 pounds since I had first met her. Bitch this, Bitch that...as I went on about how I was working and hustling more hours than her a week.

After my first book I had started working and reading a lot. I guess I was now a working pimp. I ripped into her about how the man she had loved when I met her. (Yes, the one who beat her, used her, and took her paychecks was sitting in jail indicted for murder. Over and over I yelled how I had saved her life. It could've been her instead of his new girlfriend. (Yes, the same ex-boyfriend who had told a pimp friend of mine he was going to kill me.) I guess he really did have it in him to kill. They found her (his ex) decomposed body in a suitcase in a closet. She had been missing for weeks when her family alerted police. Even though she never talked about it, I knew she must've often thought about it knowing it could've been her. But she probably still loved him. Maybe her pussy was soaked and wet as she daydreamed.

I know it sounds crazy, but you never know. I believed she still had the hots for him. Thank God, she got hired at a fast food joint and will be starting Monday. So now she'll be dancing part-time and working part-time. If she knew what I know she'd better keep that job. I have some plans of my own in the making. Damn, Iceberg Slim was right when he said, "When you start pimping, you really have join a hate club that you just can't quit."

Now I know my future, I know my destiny.

They say people get caught up thinking what they do is who they are. I was really starting to second-guess that. Was pimping my destiny? Would I ever live and lay next to a woman who didn't go out and get money from men? A woman who wakes up and gets the children ready for school. Cooks breakfast and then wakes you up with warm and wet kisses before you and her get ready for another day on the 9-to-5.

For the last 15 years I've had nothing but dancers and hoes for my main women. I had parties, Lock doors, and late nights picking up ladies from work. Was that all I knew? "Hell no!" I have a CDL license. I have a certificate in Microsoft Officer User Specialist, and Certified Nursing Assistant so why the fuck was I sitting here with one foot still in the PIMP GAME?

Was I afraid to quit?

Why was I afraid of commitment?

Why didn't I stay married to the best woman I ever knew in the world?

Why, why, damn, motherfucker, why?

Well, at least I can thank Baby-Doll for pissing me off! It propelled me to start writing this second book. I had been trying to start it for months. Anger and hate motivated me to write the poem like the one in PATERSON PIMP. It motivated me to write my first book.

Now at 4:30 A.M., anger and hate had motivated me to start writing this one. Damn, I really need therapy to help me with this "hating women shit". I want to love. I want to care. I want to feel and touch love. But I just can't! I just don't know how.

Well, before I take you on a journey in my book here's

to all my fans, to all the readers in the world, and to everyone who needs love.

I, Randy Jackson a.k.a Jashon, son of an illiterate father and raised in a Jehovah Witness cult by his mother, I would like to say: "I love you, I love you, I love all of you."

Damn! That was hard!

CHAPTER 2

SQUARE ASS NIGGA

WHEN I OPENED my eyes in the morning the first thing that popped in my mind was this Indian Princess that was coming to my party to strip tonight. It was the summer of 1999. My Go-Go business and my pimping was in full stride. It had been a good year of pimping in the safety zone (stripper clubs). But tonight was special because I had a new turnout coming to lose her virginity in the Go-Go World. Most girls start off dancing and before long their doing everything from A-Z. What woman is going to dance all night for dollars? Then her girlfriend turns one trick and makes the same or more in ten minutes. The odds were against her if she stays in the game. I've seen it happen hundreds of times. So take it from "Jashon" a brother with years and years of experience. When your girl tells you she just dancing and lap dancing nine out of ten times she lying. Too many times brothers have said to me, "Jashon, don't let my girl do nothing, but dance." I'd smile and look them dead in the eye and lie. I'm a businessman. I'm out to make as much money as I can. Shit, I'm selling every part of her except the tacks in her Go-Go boots.

Anyway, back to the story.

I had been introduced to the Indian Princess by one of my dancers named China Doll. China Doll was a Foxy Brown look-a-like. I had been introduced to China Doll by a close friend of mine named Barbara. When China Doll started living with me she would tell me how she had been a secretary for Bad Boy Entertainment in New York. She would always tell me how she knew this rapper and that rapper. But one day we were all in my apartment chilling: me, China Doll, Mrs. AC, Cholanta, and Wet-Wet, when someone told me there was a SUV outside looking for China Doll. I knew her family had been trying to get her back home for months. Anyway, she went outside and when she came back in the house she told me it was Sister Souljah trying to talk her into going back home. But at that time China Doll was too wrapped up in the Go-Go World and everything that goes along with it.

The Indian Princess was sexy as could be. She was mixed with Indian and Black and had a nice paper bag tan complexion and long black shiny hair down her back. She was about 5'6" maybe one hundred twenty-five pounds with a nice big little butt, if you know what I mean. I had taken her to the PaceMaker Go-Go Bar in Irvington, New Jersey, a couple of times just to get a feel for it and to see how the other strippers worked. But tonight was the night she was breaking luck. I knew what time I had to pick up the Indian Princess; we had set the time the day before. She had told me she needed to make 300 dollars to pay her rent. With what I had in store for her and the way she looked 300 hundred dollars would be a drop in the bucket. She told me she had a man but he wasn't trying to help her so she would help herself. I didn't give a fuck about him I was use to dealing with Square Ass Niggas all the time in this game.

Around noon I started getting calls from a strange number. Every hour on the hour this number kept appearing. Why I didn't answer it I'll never know to this day I wished I would've. It was almost time to leave for the party, Cholanta and Mrs. AC's aunt who was staying with us for the summer and was dancing for extra money and Dee-Dee were riding with me. I had sent Wet-Wet, China Doll with Mrs. AC to do another party. I should've known it was a bad luck night or a full moon when I picked Dee-Dee up and her father ran out the house as I pulled off with a baseball bat. He didn't want her going stripping with me. I laughed at the thought of that old man wanting to go upside my head with a baseball bat for trying to help his daughter get paid for her services. He should have been hitting her in the head for years for fucking men for free. He should've wanted to knock some sense in her head. Shit, he was feeding and clothing her two kids while she ran the streets fucking for free. Shit, I was trying to help him. I had everybody with me now and we were on our way to Bergen County to pick up the Indian Princess. Damn I wished I knew who this was that kept calling me all day. When I made a left onto her block her house was on the left. At first, I saw her run out the house waving her hands like the starter at a car race. She was signaling me to keep going. I made a left into her driveway. That's when I saw *him*—a big, black brother about 6'3" and two hundred and thirty pounds. He had a baldhead with muscles ripping out his tank top. My Indian Princess was saying something so I rolled my window down. She was screaming, "Jashon, I was trying to call you all day to tell you he found out about me going to the party." She continued to yell, "Leave Jashon, just leave!" As the Mr. T look-a-like approached my car the three bitches with me were yelling for me to pull off. As I tried to reverse out of the driveway he grabbed my car door and said, "I need to talk to you." Now I didn't have my gun or my knife with me, but I often do, but I had my police black jack under my front seat, but I couldn't reach it. I told Mr. T to let me park and I would get out and talk to him. As I reversed out the driveway he ran to his BMW and opened the trunk. The bitches were really screaming now to pull off. Shit, I didn't need three bitches telling me what to do. I floored the gas pedal and took off like a rocket. After five or six turns I found Teaneck Road and we figured we were home free.

As we rode down Teaneck Road laughing and joking I sparked up the weed and we were all drinking Hennessy. When all of a sudden, the BMW cut me off at a light. It was Mr. T and we were face-to-face. The left rear of his car was blocking my path. He told me that I had his wife dancing and if I came back to his house he would fuck me up or hunt me down in Paterson. Now I couldn't let him disrespect me in front of my ladies. I'm supposed to be their protector. I roared back at him. "Listen Jack, do you see any chains on anybody in this car with me? This shit is by choice not by force." Then I added fuel to the fire. I said, "With a nice car like that I'm sure you got 300 hundred dollars because that's all your woman needed." For a quick moment we stared at each other in silence. I had my left hand wrapped around the black jack like it was a winning lottery ticket. And then he broke the silence. He said, "I know you and where you're from. Don't come back to my house." and then he pulled off in a cloud of smoke with tires spinning and burning rubber. When the smoke cleared I pulled off. *What a night*, I thought. First, Dee-Dee's father wanted to crack my skull with a baseball bat and now this pussy whipped giant.

Finally I was on the way to the party one girl short, but I didn't give a fuck after all this bullshit. We started smoking weed and drinking again. As I was driving down Teaneck Road, at this moment, I was saying anybody who wanted this job or to be a pimp was crazy. Then I heard loud sirens getting louder and louder. I looked in the rearview mirror and saw about 10 unmarked and marked police cars. *Damn*, I thought to myself somebody done did something wrong because they sending the whole force after them. I pulled over to let them pass. Passing me was the last thing they were doing. They surrounded my car and jumped out with guns drawn. They were knelt down shielding themselves behind their cars. They blocked off traffic in both directions. Over the intercom they ordered me to turn the car off and throw the keys out the window. They told me to hold my hand out the window where they could see them. The girls were going hysterical. I had no clue what was going on. One thing I was certain of it wasn't a moving violation. They ordered us all out of the car and demanded us to lay flat on the ground on our face. Now don't forget it's summertime and we're on the way to a bachelor party so the girls were half naked for the party: mini-skirts and halters and thongs and heels on. We were right in front of a diner and all the patrons were staring out the window. People were coming out their houses. It was complete chaos. The cops were ram shacking my vehicle. They were inside the car and in the trunk going through the girls' bags. I was growing more and more impatient. I tried to rise to my knees to ask them what was going on. I was shoved back to the ground. All the cops were white, not one brother in the crew.

Finally after what seemed like ages I was snatched up. One of the cops asked me, "Where is it?" I said, "Where is what?" He said, "I'm going to ask you one more time. Where is it?" And I said sarcastically, "Where is what?" Then he dropped a bombshell on me that would shine some light on the whole thing. He told me that someone had made a call to the police station stating that I had pulled a gun on them. In an instant I knew what had happened. It was the Square Ass Nigga! I sighed relieved as I explained to the officer that I was a promoter and the ladies with me were dancers. I continued to explain how I had come over here to pick up a girl I had met through a friend when her jealous boyfriend and me exchanged words. One cop who was going through the ladies bags in my trunk yelled over to the cop with me and said, "He ain't lying. They are on their way to a bachelor party." he continued by saying, "There ain't nothing back here in these bags but G-strings, thongs, stilettos, and strapped on dildos and condoms, and go-go outfits." All the cops started laughing as their partner held up a pair of 9 inch heeled thigh high boots in one hand and a cat woman outfit in the other hand.

As everything settled down the cops apologized to me and explained that they had to follow a certain protocol for all suspected gun calls. They tried hard to get me to come back to the police station and file a report and press charges on the Square Ass Nigga, but I declined. They were very angry with him for making a fake call. I never even knew it was illegal. But they were taking it serious and really wanted me to make a complaint. I just wanted to get to the bachelor party.

As the girls tried to sort their stuff out and put it back together I knew I still had a problem. I had dropped a bag of weed between the seats before I got out of the car. And we were drinking Hennessy too. As the cop that was searching the car approached me all I could think of was how tight he would put the handcuffs on my wrists. But he didn't have his handcuffs out. He extended his hand to shake my hand. I stuck my hand out to shake his hand. I felt something in my hand as he said, "Enjoy yourself and be careful tonight and sorry for the inconvenience." As I walked to the car I looked down at my hand and to my amazement it was the bag of weed. It was only a nickel bag of weed so I guess it was the least they could do. Well, we did finally make it to the party and the girls made a lot of money that night. But after all these years, I think I know what happened that night. The Indian Princess never wanted to strip. She played me and used me to make her jealous boyfriend cough up the 300 hundred dollars. Reason being he knew too much about me. He knew my name. He knew where I was from. Also what time I was coming. He knew too much. See she probably told him if he didn't give it to her she would get it herself. But her plans backfired when I never answered their calls that day and just showed up.

She did call me days later to say how sorry she was. I screamed into the phone, "BITCH, I'M A PIMP NOT A RELATIONSHIP THERAPIST AND I WANT YOU AND YOUR SQUARE ASS NIGGA TO STAY THE FUCK AWAY FROM ME!" I was laughing as I slammed down the phone. But I'll always remember the "Indian Princess" and how beautiful she was. Damn, she could have made me some money! And I know nine out of ten men who would've wanted to kill over that fine bitch!

CHAPTER 3

ATLANTIC CITY DANIELLE

I WAS LAYING back in my bed at the Resorts Casino and Hotel, when I heard fumbling at the door. Those damn card keys they use to enter doors now never seem to work with the first swipe. Whoever was at the door was having a hell of a time trying to get in. No doubt it was Baby-Doll. She was always in and out of the hotel room when we would be in Atlantic City. She loved it down there. It would be her home away from home. It also was a break from those sweaty ass Go-Go bars she worked in every night bringing money home for her man. When she worked that bitch worked with the militancy of a dedicated soldier. And when she chilled like down in Atlantic City where we would frequent at least once a month she would chill at the bars, boardwalk, dining and even get massages—all this she would do alone 95% of the time, unless Playboy would come with his moneymaker. Then they would hang together and Playboy would be out on Pacific Ave stalking hoes and I would relax in my hotel room.

My interests were in resting and dressing and pimping my black ass off. Playboy would always fill the hotel room with the sweet, but stank odor of sex as soon as we stepped foot in the hotel room. I would shake my head and laugh, as he would tell me he had to fuck his bitch before he sent her out to get money. His beliefs were it always got his bitch engine running and she would definitely make money for him before she returned. I would always laugh and tell him he was pimping backwards. But the bitch always came back with money so I guess he knew his bitch inside and out.

The door opened and it was Baby-Doll. She was excited. For one quick second I thought she had hit the jackpot at the slot machine in the casino or something. That thought was broke with "Daddy, Daddy," she was saying over and over. "What Bitch," I said. "Remember, Danielle?" she asked. I said, "Who?" She said, "Danielle, baby." Danielle was a chick Baby-Doll had met on the track in Atlantic City months ago on one of our previous visits. I had spoke with her briefly about joining our family but she had got away from me that time. Baby-Doll said, "Danielle is sleeping down in the bus depot." I roared, "Go get that bitch then before she leaves again!"

When the door closed I jumped out of bed and went to the bathroom to get sexy. I brushed my teeth, washed my face, and brushed my hair. I rubbed coco butter on my face until it glowed. I sprayed my braids with new shine. I put on my velour white robe with my navy blue silk boxers and matching navy blue fluffy slippers. I looked in the mirror, even though I was 42 at the time and my hair was started to recede and thin out a little. I was still a sexy chocolate pimp.

When Baby-Doll entered the room with Danielle they sat at the table. I sat in the middle of the bed in between the two double beds facing them. Danielle looked like shit. Her clothes were filthy and her hair, what little she had was in desperate need of a wash and a perm. Thinking about a weave or anything else at this time was comical. This was going to be an easy cope as she sat there looking at Baby-Doll in amazement. I winked at Baby-Doll for her to start with the how good I was. How much money *she* could make. In 30 days with my Daddy and me your life will be new and improved.

Baby-Doll and me had run this down on plenty bitches in four and a half years together. Even though she told me she had a drug habit I decided I would chance it with her. Danielle asked Baby-Doll for a cigarette as they sat at the table. I turned around and reached for my lighter. When I turned back around Baby-Doll was sitting there but the bitch Danielle had done a Houdini. She was gone. I looked at Baby-Doll and she looked at me. I followed her eyes to the floor; Danielle was on the floor in a Muslim prayer position with her face flat on the floor like she was licking the carpet. I rushed around the bed, she wasn't moving. I called her name over and over but nothing. I turned her over on her back she was out cold and sucking every breath like it was her last. My brain was racing. I couldn't let this bitch die in my room. My name was on the marquee at the front desk. I didn't know what drugs she had taken before she arrived. Baby-Doll was running around the room in a panic: "Should I call 911, Daddy?" she asked. I screamed. "HELL NO!" My days as an orderly in those two hospitals when I was young kicked in. I grabbed the ice bucket and rushed out the door like it was a fire. I filled the bucket with ice and ran back to the room. Baby-Doll opened the door on my first knock. I rushed over to the lifeless corpse on the floor. Damn, she pissed on herself. I always knew people go to the bathroom on themselves right before they die. I snatched her pants open and zipped her zipper down. Mouth to mouth was nowhere on my mind. Now that was out of the question! I dumped the bucket of ice down her pants in the crotch area. Like magic the bitch started flapping around and jerking like a fish out of water. I gave her one hard slap, POW, her eyes popped wide open. After about ten minutes she was sitting up in a chair like nothing had happened. She didn't even remember. Baby-Doll and me packed our shit and the three of us ran out of that hotel room like runaway slaves. The ride back to Paterson was terrible. That bitch had my car smelling like dead fish, piss, and vomit. She would need a complete makeover before she could hit the streets to make my money.

When we arrived at Baby-Doll's apartment I knew I was in trouble. Before we could get out of the car Danielle asked me if I could get her a hit of crack cocaine. The bitch hadn't even showered yet. Two days later she would pass out again. This time I took her to the hospital where she would spend eight days. I had Baby-Doll visiting her and bringing her outside food everyday too. When she came home it took another week before she gained all her strength back. It was almost a month before she finally hit the streets to work. I had gone shopping for her and dressed her up to the best of my ability. This is the part of the pimp game that many people never knew about. The ups and the downs, and this was most definitely a down part. I had been feeding and sheltering a hoe for a whole month and hadn't received a dime yet!

28-Randy Jackson a.k.a Jashon

The night she hit the hoe stroll I was happy. I could finally start getting money back on this investment. The first couple of nights went well and I was starting to feel like this had been a good business move. Baby-Doll was in the bars getting money and Danielle was in the streets. During the second week I noticed money was getting shorter and shorter. And when I talked to Danielle she would look away in another direction. So I got a friend of mine to start keeping his eye on her while she worked the streets. Finally during the third week it was evident the bitch was smoking crack again. And I found out from my friend that every time she turned a trick she did the 100-yard dash to the crack house. That night when she left for work she never came back. About three weeks later my friend would tell me where she was camping out. I knocked on the door and a cracked out zombie came to the door with fangs for teeth. I asked for Danielle. When Danielle came to the door she looked worse than the night I met her in Atlantic City. To my surprise, she still had on a leather jacket I had bought her to hoe in. I snatched it off her back and threw five dollars on the ground as I walked away. The zombie looking bitch and her jumped on the ground fighting for the five-dollar bill. As I walked off the porch I told her to, "Keep up the bad work." The only reason I tossed the five dollars to her was so she wouldn't call the cops on me for snatching back the coat I bought.

To this day she is still on Broadway cracked out looking like death. What would make a woman choose to be homeless, hungry, dirty and broke? I don't know but that's the question I asked myself every time I see Danielle on Broadway. To this day she still waves at me as I drive by. Pimpin' ain't easy.

CHAPTER 4

OH, SHIT! IT'S MY COUSIN!

IT WAS BLACK JESUS, KEY-OF-LIFE, MASTER SAVIOR, SIR ALLAH, and me, were sitting on my porch listening to the boom box. We were getting high as giraffes. I believe the year was 1980 or 1981, as the Old English beer went round and round. And we passed around joint after joint of some good ass weed from a spot in Harlem that was called "Boogie Wonderland".

We had gold, red, and mixed weed from the spot. Black Jesus and I couldn't stop talking about what we had seen earlier.

I was driving my moped down Park Ave with Black Jesus on the back when we approached 31st Street. When I got to the corner of 31st Street, I saw what looked like a soccer ball falling from the sky. Then cars stopped and people screamed. I stopped and Black Jesus jumped off the back and ran around the corner to see what had happened. What I thought was a soccer ball ended up being a baby. A woman had thrown her infant baby off the 5th floor balcony and then jumped herself. The baby died upon impact but the woman lived.

The story made headlines. The next day I found out the scoop. Apparently, the woman was a mistress to a doctor and had his child. After he refused to leave his wife, the distraught woman had tried double-suicide. Half her plan worked. The baby died and she became paralyzed from the neck down. So as we told the crew about the tragic accident we had seen earlier that day, a station wagon pulled up. It was more of the homey's. So just like in the movie *Cooley High* we all jumped in the stolen car. Ready for a night of joy riding. We rode around for hours, drinking and smoking, and taken turns driving. As day turned to night we were starting to get bored with just driving around. So we decided to go to Eastside Park and give the car a break. So we parked and got out and begin smoking and drinking some more.

It had to be at least eight of us in that station wagon. I guess we were a little too loud because we started to notice a couple of porch lights pop on. So we jumped in the station wagon and took off. But before we could leave the park we spotted *them*. Two gay guys were walking into the park with blankets. Someone said, "Look at those two fags. Let's fuck 'em up."

In a split second we went from joy riding to getting ready to commit what is called today a "hate crime". A hate crime that was punishable with up to 25-50 years.

The driver made a U-turn and shut of the headlights. We circled around. We wanted to catch 'em far enough from the entrance so there escape was slim. As we approached 'em we slowed down to maybe 5 miles per hour. The two were so busy talking I don't even know if they paid the long station wagon any attention. It was nighttime and I'm sure they could not see us in the car. They probably assumed it was two people engaging in sexual acts.

As we prepared to jump out I heard, "Ready?"

"Yeah, you ready?"

"Yeah ok, let's do this shit. Let's fuck 'em up."

"OH SHIT," I yelled.

"What J? Hold up. What J?"

"OH SHIT! IT'S MY COUSIN!" One of the guys was my cousin. "It's my cousin," I said again. "Pull off, pull off!" The driver put the pedal to the medal and we took off.

First, I would like to say I have nothing against homosexuals. That was just another time when being young and dumb and almost allowing peer pressure to fuck my life up. With 8 high out of their minds thugs jumping on two men, we could've killed 'em.

Lesson to be learned of how a joy ride in a stolen car almost turned into an assault or attempted murder charge. I never told my cousin about this. And he never knew how close he'd come to a vicious attack that night in Eastside Park!

CHAPTER 5

LOVE GONNA GET YOU 'CAUSE BITCHES AIN'T SHIT!

HER NAME WAS FELICA. And I'll never forget her.

The year was '88, I believe. I was a married man living a square life. I was an orderly at a hospital in Paterson. And I also had a part-time job as a bus operator. My two sons (by my wife) were 5 and 2 at the time. I was working in the intensive care unit of the hospital. At this time I was happy with my marriage and happy with my job. Even though my wife was a brilliant woman and a dream come true, I still had a wandering eye and taste for different pussy, occasionally. I'm not sure what makes a man cheat when he's happy at home. I guess it's just an animal instinct inside of you to conquer as much pussy as you can, by any means necessary. Even at the risk of breaking up and losing your children and family.

Anyway, I had seen Felica on many occasions. She was light-skinned with shoulder length hair. She was about 5'1". Maybe 135 pounds with a nice fat round ass. Her titties were full and round and stood up like she was a teenager. I was 25 years old. She must've been no more than 21. She had moved to Paterson from Atlanta, Georgia.

We would always speak to each other in our daily meetings at the job. I could tell she had the hots for me after about her first month on the job. One day I struck up a conversation and it seemed like we had known each other forever. Here I was married and she was living with her man. It was perfect for nothing but a sex relationship, which was fine with me because I wasn't leaving my family at this time for nothing in the world.

Felica would tell me how much her man loved her all the time. Every week we had the same day off and we would meet and go to the hotel and fuck our brains out. But as soon as we were done, she would lay there and become depressed and sad. She would tell me that she didn't know why she cheated on her man when he loved her so much. I would dose in and out of sleep as she lay on my chest and tell me over and over again how she didn't know why she was doing what she was doing because her man loved her so much.

It was approaching our day off and all Felica had been telling me since the last time we fucked was how she had a surprise for me when we fuck the next time. When I picked her up in the morning I knew I was in for some real serious fucking. She had on a mini-skirt with no panties on. The cleavage that was showing would have made any man's dick hard.

"You ready Daddy," she said, as she jumped in the car and pulled my dick out and starting jerking it. Her hands felt like they were made to jerk dick. Up and down, up and down...she must've had grease on her palms before she got in. The smell of her soft but arousing perfume and the way she stroked my dick had my dick rock hard. I had to wait 15 minutes before I could go pay for the hotel room with *her* money. My dick was so hard. This was one horny country nasty fine ass red bitch!

After I paid (rather she paid) for the room from the car to the hotel door she was constantly touching me somewhere. It kept me rock hard.

Now I don't have the longest dick in the world. But in width my dick is fat. And she was going to get all that fat dick in her throat and pussy today!

When the door closed I pushed her down to her knees and pushed my dick in her mouth. She began deep-throating it. Then she would suck the head, and then back to deep-throating it—back and forth. Then she would lick the head and the sides from the head to my pubic hairs. She started sucking the head like she was trying to suck every drop of cum out, but I wasn't cumming. I bend down and picked her up and carried her to the bed. I laid her down and started licking and sucking her nipples with my finger playing with her clit. Then I began kissing her on the neck and around her ears, and around her hairline. I turned her over and began kissing and licking the back of her kneecaps and under her butt cheeks. I turned her back over and squeezed her titties together and licked her nipples one at a time. Then I kissed her all the way down from her nipples, down her stomach, toward her pussy. I kissed her left inner thigh, and then her right inner thigh, back and forth, left to right and every time I passed her clit I licked it lightly driving her crazy and wild. Then without notice I stuck my tongue in her pussy and started sucking and licking her pussy and clit. When she climaxed she screamed and tried to run, but I held her legs tight and licked her clit—fast and furiously. Then I rose up and shoved my fat dick into her pussy and pounded that tight wet pussy until I bust. When I bust I snatched my dick out and came all over her titties and stomach.

Before she could start with that "my man love me so much shit" I drifted off to sleep. When I woke up she was talking about the surprise she had for me. She told me to turn over on my stomach. I wanted to know for what. But she just kept saying, "Turn over, turn over." So I turned over and she pulled my ass open, I spun around and asked her, "What you doing?" She said, "You never had your ass licked?" and I said, "Hell, no!" she said, "Well, this will be your first time and I guarantee you'll like it." I turned back over, not knowing what to expect. She pulled my ass open and began licking my ass. I won't say how it felt but I'll say it was different. And she was the first to ever lick it.

The first thing I thought about when she was done was that the bitch didn't even brush her teeth or gargle or wash her face. I gargled and brushed my teeth before we left. Why she didn't, I didn't know. We both had someone at home.

As I approached her block, she said I could drop her off in front of her house because today her man wasn't supposed to be there. But as we got closer to the house he was getting out of his car so I kept going and let her out at the corner. When she got out I didn't pull off I waited and watched from my rearview mirror. He spotted her coming up the street. He was smiling from ear to ear. Yes, he was in love with her and it showed all over his face. The closer she got the bigger his smile got. Then it happened...they embraced and he gave her a big long tongue kiss. They kissed; I couldn't believe that that bitch kissed him after licking my ass 30 minutes ago and she didn't even brush her teeth. I'll never forget that as long as I live. Yes, and whenever I hear that record by KRS1, I think of that day. LOVE GONNA GET YOU ('Cause Bitches Ain't Shit!).

CHAPTER 6

BOOTA...I THOUGHT IT WAS A MARCHING BAND!

IT WAS A BEAUTIFUL sunny summer day. My brother, Silky had just bought a spanking new Caprice Classic, white on white with a burgundy half vinyl top. The year was maybe 1989, I think. Our plans were to pick up these two young hoes from the projects. We had chilled with them on several occasions—just kicking pimp talk and getting high. Today was the day we were hoping they would choose. Choose us as their pimps so we could put them down and start letting them suck and fuck our pockets fat. So we picked them up, got some drinks, and headed to New York to get some Boota. Boota was high-powered reefer that everyone was smoking at this time. On the way to New York the radio was jamming hit after hit, the kind of music when it feels like the DJ was playing the records just for you. By the time we crossed the GW Bridge, Silky and me were tapping each other and winking at each other. As we pulled up in front of the Boota spot, I was on cloud nine. I got out of the car and stuck my head through the back window and kissed the bitch on the cheek and whispered in her ear, "Daddy will be right back." Then I stuck my tongue in her ear like I thought it could come out of the other side. She broke out in laughter and grabbed her ears with both her hands, and just kept squeezing her face between her hands and shaking like she was having an orgasm. As I walked away I thought to myself, *yes, that move would surely fuck her head up.*

Earlier my brother Silky had given her girlfriend a dozen roses at the gas station when we stopped for gas. The bitch cried for 15 minutes straight saying no one had ever given her shit. Roses from a gas station ain't that some shit!

Well, anyway, back to the story.

As I pushed the door open to the building I started taking two stairs at a time on my way to the 5th floor. I was in a hell of a hurry to get that Boota and get back to my soon to be money tree in the car. I wanted to fill her brain with Boota and maybe, just maybe, I could've had her on the track tonight. Rather her girlfriend would be with her or not that was up to her and Silky. What her girlfriend ate didn't make her shit. When I got to the 5th floor, I approached 5G, and knocked three times. This dude opened the peephole and said, "What do you need?"

I said, "Ten bags of Boota," and slid my money through the peephole. As he pushed my bags through the tiny peephole to me one of the bags fell to the floor, as I bent down to pick it up, for a moment it sounded like I heard the pitter-patter of a marching band boots against the ground.

    Anyway, I picked up the bag and stuffed all 10 bags in my pockets and started running back down the stairs 4 at a time. The closer I got to the ground floor, the louder the boots of the marching band sounded. Those boots pounded against the pavement and were sending off a sweet cadence. Where were the drums, I wondered, as I opened the door? Oh shit! Oh shit! I said to myself. There were SWAT trucks outside the building. The sounds I had heard were from the police officers jumping out the back of those SWAT trucks and running down the street toward the building I was leaving out of.

    Now, here was where I been kicking myself in the ass for years over my next move. Now me not being from New York and not thinking, but thinking like a young snot nose punk with no smarts came in. When I stuck my head out the door I should've just walked out like I was one of the 1,000 to maybe 3, 000 tenants in the large tall building. They wouldn't have ever suspected anything other than me being another tenant. They were on the way in the building to raid the Boota spot. Instead I stuck my head out the door and just as they approached the door I slammed it shut in their faces and spun around and started running back up the stairs. Don't ask me why or where I was running. I didn't know anyone in the building. But the Boota spot door and I was from New Jersey, anyway. Now I was running back up the stairs 6 at a time. Flight after flight with the SWAT team right on my heels. I remembered feeling fingertips on my collar as I spun to hit another staircase. I heard what sounded like a ladies voice. Damn, it was a female officer and two male officers chasing me and they were white. The other SWAT team had stopped on the 5th floor of the Boota spot. When I reached the top it seemed like I had just ran to the top of the Empire State Building. There was a door to the roof, no doubt. As I reached out and hit it with my shoulder, DAMN, it was locked! Good thing it was, because they might have thrown me off the roof. Shit, I didn't know when the three SWAT officers reached for me. I fell down in a fetal position as they kicked and stomped and punched me for about 10 minutes, non-stop. Then one of them grabbed me by the neck and dragged me down to the Boota spot door. There were cops on both sides of the spot's door with guns drawn, as they banged on the door over and over again. Then they did something I'll never forget as long as I live. They held me in front of the door by my neck and kept pounding on the door with my nose pressing against the same peephole I had slid my money in to get the Boota. Over and over they pounded on the door. "Police, open up," they repeated. If the dealers would have shot through the door I would have been dead. The cops would have probably said I died in a drug deal that had gone bad.

After about 10 minutes, they moved me from the peephole and knocked the door open. To my amazement, the apartment was empty. They probably went out the window, down the fire escape or went roof to roof and were smoking a spliff and laughing at the cops.

The police began questioning me. I told them I was from Jersey. I still had the Boota in my pocket. I was trying to say I was visiting a friend when they pulled the Boota out of my pocket. The young white lady cop smacked the shit outta me. And then told me to get rid of it. I was still dazed from the smack. So I started to walk away with the Boota. *Smack*, one of them had hit me in the back of the head, grabbed one bag and ripped it open and said, "Get rid of it." So I ripped open one bag at a time and poured it on the floor in the building. After that I staggered out of the building sore and soaked from sweating, and dazed from the ass whooping New York's finest put on me.

When I stepped outside Silky was gone. I walked around the corner, up and down, back and forth, for what seemed like an hour. SWAT had, no doubt scared him away, but where did he go? Where, to the moon? Then I spotted Silky and the two bitches, the looks on their faces let me know how bad I must've looked. I fell down in the front seat. The bitches were asking me over and over what happened. Silky asked me did I get the Boota. He said was ready to get high because he had been driving around for hours.

As I lay back and closed my eyes all I kept thinking over and over and over in my mind was that damn Boota and that I thought it was a MARCHING BAND!

CHAPTER 7

JUMP, BITCH, JUMP!

IP AND ME HAD BEEN out slumming all day. It was no different from any other day. We were hitting Spanish people left and right in Passaic. At this time in the early 90s Passaic was a little Puerto Rico. And for some reason Hispanics who loved gold or "audo" as they called it—all day slumming. All you would hear was "to getta audo my friend, that fantasy, this no fantasy, test it, test it, its gold all the way through, get some bleach, dip it in battery acid." They would say. Or sometimes they would even pull a string of hair out of their head to see if it stuck to the gold. They had so many ways of trying to test that fake shit we sold. No matter what it always got sold? IP was so good we had named him King Slump. He had in returned named me Cheap Slump, because once I got my money back that I had spent at the fake jewelry spot, which was called Oh Jewelry or John's, I would let my slump go for anything. My reasoning was this: if I spent a $100.00 on fake shit. Once I sold enough and got my $100.00 back everything after that was profit so I would ask for $200.00 and take 5 dollars if they had it. So IP named me Cheap Slump. And IP named Mike Nice (aka Just-I) Keep Slump because at the end of the day he always had more slump left, which meant IP or I-Power (as most called him) and I would joke on him all night. Because, no matter what, all slump had to go, you never wanted to wake up the next day with a piece of slump. Well, maybe one piece to hit someone to help with gas money or the toll to New York. The night before we probably spent our money on weed, cocaine, bitches and the motel. Oh yeah, and a new outfit from head to toe if it was the weekend. Maybe a down payment on some jewelry too, a nameplate, four-finger ring or name rings.

Well, anyway, back to the story.

We had just left 164th Street and Broadway in Manhattan. Back in those days the coke was great fish scale rock I mean raw with a capital R. It could take several cuts if you wanted to cut it. Anyway, that day we decided to sniff it raw. No lactose, which was used to cut coke to make more and bring down the potency so it wouldn't burn a whole in your nose or overdose if you shot it directly in your veins. As we hit the exit for Paterson off Route 80, we felt relieved. That ride from New York to Paterson on Route 80 was always tense and stressful when you had a pocket full of drugs like weed and coke in your lap. Once we hit Paterson we were home and felt safe. We stopped at a liquor store to get some drinks and some E-Z Wider to roll up some weed. As we pulled up we spotted them at the same time...three young hot sexy black chicks. Well, 2 of them were hot you know one in the crew was always ugly or fat. Females always kept one with them like that. I don't know why. Maybe the bitch could fight or scared off dudes the fine bitches didn't want to fuck with. I didn't know. I really didn't give a fuck, either because I'd talk to an ugly fat bitch in a minute. And have her giving me her paychecks every week. And all my partners know that about me. And most fat and ugly chicks have low self-esteem, but don't get me wrong some hold their head up high and don't take any shit. And if you have a problem with their weight or something they would tell you to go fuck yourself. But I always thought it was just more cushion for the pushin'.

Anyway, me and IP jumped right on them telling them we got weed and drinks and coke, "Let's go hang out." and like magic all three jumped in my backseat and we took off. Now we were parked behind an elementary school in Paterson. I believe School #20; the same one IP and me went to. My car radio was blasting and we were smoking and drinking and me and IP were feeling like we hit the jackpot and I guessed they were looking at us like that too, thinking they had free get high all night. Then we pulled out the coke and started sniffing. Two of the girls' eyes almost jumped out of their head. They were smiling from ear to ear. Now sharing weed and beer was one thing, but letting them sniff up our coke was another.

Now they were on the fucking side of the menu. We decided to pass it around and around and around the coke went. It was the fat ugly chick that wouldn't sniff the coke; no doubt she was the watchdog for the crew. After about 1 or 2 hours it was time to get rid of one of those chicks so we could hit some cheap motel on Route 46 like the Airport motel. So we all jumped back in my car and started riding. I had noticed the slim chick acting kinda weird when we were getting high behind the school. She was running around climbing the backstop gate to the baseball field, running the bases like she had hit a homerun, but I thought she was just having fun. I didn't care how much she ran and jumped as long as she jumped on my dick before the night was over. I didn't give a fuck, as much of my coke she sniffed. As I drove down Park Ave, I heard her say something like I feel like jumping out this car. She was in the back on the passenger side behind IP who was in the front passenger seat. The fat broad was behind me and the other chick was in the middle. Then she said it again, "I feel like jumping out of this car. I feel like jumping out of this motherfucking car!" IP and me looked at each other and started laughing. Then she said it again, "I'ma jump out this motherfucking car." So IP said, "Jump, bitch, jump!" I said, "Don't jump out this car, bitch!" IP was screaming, "Jump, bitch, jump!" And I kept screaming, "Don't jump out of this car, bitch!" and she was screaming, "I'ma jump out this car motherfucker!" It was crazy. We were all screaming at the same time over and over, "Jump bitch, don't jump, bitch, I'ma jump, I'ma jump, I'ma jump!" Her girlfriends were screaming and holding her left arm. It was complete chaos in the car. I made a right off of Park Ave and 23rd Street heading toward School #13, then a right. I should've pulled over or stayed on the street with the stop sighs. As I drove down 15th Ave everyone was still yelling and screaming, the bitch had her right hand on the door handle. I guessed that uncut raw coke had her speeding. I was driving about 45 miles per hour and then it happened. I heard the door handle as she pulled it, the last thing I heard as I reached back with my right hand into the backseat was IP saying, "I don't give a fuck. Jump, bitch, jump." She opened the door and jumped like she was diving off a diving board. It was like in a movie when someone was hanging off a cliff and they had a hold of someone's hand trying to hold them and then they fall. I felt my fingertips brush her body as she leaped out of the car. I jerked back and looked in my rearview mirror. She looked like a rag doll bouncing and rolling as her body pounded the pavement, over and over. Her 2 friends were screaming for me to stop. I was in a state of shock. IP was, well, IP was IP. I refused to go back. I was letting her 2 friends out to go back and check on her. As I let them out and pulled off I noticed there was a car following me. We didn't know who it was. I told IP to try to see if it was an unmarked police car. No, it was two old ladies following me. We decided to try and dip on them, but every turn I made, they made. We decided to stop and find out what they wanted. I pulled over as the two senior citizen ladies pulled up beside me and said, "Why did you throw that girl out of your car. She could have been killed!" I tried to explain to them that she jumped out at her own free will. But they didn't believe me. They said that they were going to give my plate number to the police. *Damn*, I thought. The cops would never believe me. I was pissed with IP for coaching the bitch to jump.

Anyway, days went by, then weeks, and then months, and now it's been years. I guessed the old ladies changed their minds or their story sounded too farfetched, but this was really crazy. Over the years I have seen that chick hundreds of times: in the streets, in stores, everywhere and she didn't even remember me. Or perhaps, she didn't want to remember me. But I'll never forget that one summer night when that bitch jumped out of my car while I was driving. I think that was one of the craziest nights IP and me ever had together and we've had many.

Jump, bitch, jump!

CHAPTER 8

PHILADELPHIA BOB

MY PHONE RANG with a strange number. Whenever my phone rang with a number I didn't know, it would usually meant a party, which meant *money*. It was a white man voice on the other end. "Hello, what's your fantasy, Jashon speaking." I was hoping this wasn't another pathetic trick about to ask me a million questions that wouldn't lead to anything. The male voice said, "I'm trying to get some dancers for this weekend." In a flash of a second my mind went from annoyed to alert. So I started with the usual: "What do you need the girls for a bachelor party? Going away present? Fight night?"

The male voice said, "It's for a bachelor party and I need five girls, no blacks either."

Ain't this a bitch!

The voice spoke again, "There'll be white and Hispanic men—cops and firemen. If you can't supply white girls, then, they would settle for Spanish."

Now first of all, in all my years I have never had a

request for no Black dancers. Even if only one, they wanted some Mandingo blood there. I've been doing this for years and one thing you never say was: I DON'T or I CAN'T, under any circumstances. Reason being: NUMBER 1: a light-skinned Black dancer can be Spanish, Chinese, Jamaican or even white or mixed once the guys have drank enough. NUMBER 2: Do you really think a room full of drunk men on the eve of their buddy's wedding night will turn down Black dancers. Huh, if they wanted Spanish or Spanish dancers, if they wanted White or whatever. Hell no!

So I had a problem now. Baby-Doll was mixed with Black and White. So she could pass for White or Spanish. I had a young 18 year old mixed with Black and Dominican so she was cool too. But I needed 3 more Spanish or White chicks. So I called a Pimp Buddy of mine named Super, and he just happened to have a Pimp Buddy in town from the city of Brotherly Love, which was Philly. His name was Philadelphia Bob, and he had two Spanish chicks dancing for him. I called him up and we talked and he agreed to bring them to the party that Friday.

Now I was set with Baby-Doll and my young mixed Dominican, and Philadelphia Bob's two Spanish strippers. I was good.

When Friday night came I was ready. Baby-Doll was looking good with her miniskirt high on those thick ass thighs with a pair of fuck me boots on. Her cleavage was so noticeable I was sure there would be many bills raining down on her this night. I had on some gators and slacks with a tailor-made button up silk shirt with my trademark Panama hat on. As I picked up my young Dominican mami I was off to pick up Philly Bob and his two girls. My fifth dancer was running late. She would have to jump in a cab and meet me there.

When I approached the address I didn't know what to expect. Then I saw them two nice looking well-built Spanish girls. The guy with them was about 5'5" inches tall. He had on a tank top and shorts with sneakers. He introduced himself as Philly Bob and said they were ready.

Now PIMPIN' has nothing to do with looks or big dicks. You can be fat and ugly with a 2-inch penis and have more game and pimping ability than the next man. But I didn't expect him to look like that especially with those two high powdered Spanish hoes.

Anyway, when we got there I didn't know what to expect with them not wanting Black dancers. Were they racist? Were they picky? I wasn't sure because I know for a fact white men have been crazy for Black pussy since slavery days so I was a little shook.

The fifth dancer I didn't care about because I could bring anybody and makeup an excuse when I got there and still get my money for the girls to dance. And danced only being it was white and Spanish cops. Both parties signed my contract when I got the deposit. At the bottom of my contract in big bold black letters it read:

ENTERTAINERS DANCE ONLY!

One thing about Philly Bob, he didn't give a fuck if they were black, white, or blue. He told me he was a hyped man who would get those white boys to spend money tonight. So I sat back and watched in amazement as he hyped the crowd. Let me tell you Flavor Flav didn't have shit on Philly Bob. If a dancer jumped on the bar, he jumped on the bar, too. If a dancer jumped on the pool table, he jumped on the pool table, too. He was jumping around that place yelling and screaming into the microphone like a chimp on fire. The white men loved him and enjoyed him as much as the shows the ladies put on that night. The ladies were setting their ass on fire with moose, pulling beads out their asshole, spitting lemons out their pussy. Yes. It was a hell of a night. White men knew how to party!

When the night was over the girls were in the dressing rooms getting dress and counting their money. I came in the room to speak to Baby-Doll. Philly Bob main women or should I say his Bottom Ho was giving me some strange looks. Now even for her to look at another Pimp, she was out-of-pocket with that reckless eyeballin'. I could have charge Philly Bob for that. But I continued to talk to my two ladies. Then I heard her say to me, "If you have anymore parties let us know. She was handing me her phone to put my number in it when Philly Bob walked in. At first, he froze, then he said in an ass pleasing voice, "Oh yeah, you can exchange numbers with her money for her means money for me." On that note I told Baby-Doll to get her number. I didn't feel right exchanging my number with her after he made that statement: "Money for her means money for me." It just didn't sit well on my stomach. And if the bitch decided to change teams he would have full responsibility for allowing her to pass off her digits to another Pimp or Bitch. To me it was pimping backwards.

After that Baby-Doll would see Philly Bob main women from time to time at different bars they danced at. She would keep me updated and I would also quiz Baby-Doll.

One of his women had bounced back to Philly, but his main Bitch stayed with him in P-town. They were no longer staying with my Pimp Buddy who had introduced us. They were staying at my man's protégé's house now.

His protégé was an upcoming PIMP in town, which should've concerned Philly Bob. Many young pimps hung over his house. I knew if his game weren't tight he would get that Bitch stolen from him before he knew what happened. Philly Bob would call me from time to time to see if I had any parties lined up. We would talk PIMP GAME for a while and then hang up.

I liked Philly Bob a lot. I remember the last conversation I had with him. I asked him was everything all right? He was in a good mood; out chilling in P-town with his bitch home in a house with other hoes and pimps. I asked him did he think that was a good idea. And I'll always remember what he said. "Jashon, my bitch ain't going nowhere, trust me." I think he even said she had his name tattooed on her or hers was tattooed on him. I can't recall but something like that.

It was a weekend night and Playboy and me were out cruising the streets of Paterson. Playboy my Pimp Buddy loved to cruise around and scream on bitches. He was ferocious when it came to screaming on bitches. His style was completely opposite of mine. I'd come like a sheep and hide my corrupt intentions behind my sexy chocolate face. And only transform into a dangerous wolf, when necessary. No one would ever know from looking at me the vicious and brutal acts I have used in my years as a pimp. And I'll never write about it either. It's nothing to be proud of. I hold lots of shame and pain inside for those acts.

Anyway, daylight was breaking through and Playboy and me had been out all night. Earlier I had picked Baby-Doll up from work and dropped her off and Playboy had sent Sex-Appeal on a couple of dates and took her home. Since 2 a.m., we had rode around trying to knock some hoes or massage some young bitches tonsils. It was 6 a.m., when I dropped Playboy off. I prayed when I got home that Baby-Doll would be asleep. Most of the time she would wait up for me or pretend to be sleep and when I'd come home if she stayed the night at my spot. When I came into the bedroom, thank god, she was asleep. As I took off my clothes, I noticed she was on her side with her back to me with that fat red ass sticking out from under the covers. Now before you think I'm a sucker man. I know this is a trick that every woman does: Ho or Bitch, Girlfriend or Wife. This is the let me see if he fucked or not trick. It usually would have pissed me off but before it did my dick popped up hard as a rock. It looked like a king cobra head. Well, I passed the test because I pulled that fat ass open, spit on my hand and rubbed it all over my fat black dick head and slowly worked my way in that warm wet pussy....

The phone woke me up. It was 8 a.m. I had just fallen asleep 15 minutes ago. What I thought would be a quickie turned into a whole hour of ecstasy and orgasms. I was sticky and wet as I answered the phone. The crying voice on the other end kept saying, "Jashon, Jashon, help me, help me. They fucked me up and took my bitch!" It was Philly Bob. He didn't know where he was in Paterson. Of course not, he was from Philly. He had been in Paterson no more than 3 months and it finally fucked him. He was somewhere downtown with nothing on but shorts and slippers. He didn't have a penny in his pockets and he was using someone's cell phone to call me. From the landmarks he gave me he was somewhere downtown on Memorial Drive by Kansas Chicken. When he got in the car I could see the embarrassment in his eyes. He was devastated and humiliated. This was the tragic side of pimping. The part you don't see on TV. The part many pimps hope they never experience. As I pulled off he began to cry as he began to tell me what had happened. It went something like this:

At the apartment he was sharing with the young pimps they were throwing a party or lock door. He had noticed his Bottom woman acting strange lately. She had begun laughing and joking around with the young pimps a lot who owned the house. He said when he would return home from errands she would often be in his room with his other ladies. I told him to hold up one minute I had to make a call. I called Playboy and said, "Pimp in Distress," we had a game that whenever one of us had pimping problems we would call each other and say, "Pimp in Distress." Anyway, he answered the phone and I told him it was important to come downstairs in 15 minutes. He said okay and hung up. With Playboy being my main man with only a few years under his belt in pimping I thought it would be good for him to hear this story so Philly Bob continued. He said his Bitch had done a date and went and sat by the young pimp (a move he said later was probably planned). When he called her she refused to move. He said he then said, "Come here, Bitch!" Philly Bob said he then walked over and slapped his bitch. That's when he said the shit broke out. Punches rain down on him from every direction—from everyone in the house. He made it out the house with just shorts and slippers on. When he finally stopped running. I guessed that's when he called me. As Playboy got in the car he repeated the whole story. Playboy knew the young pimps from the street. Philly Bob had learned a valuable lesson in pimping. Never trust another pimp. Never trust a Ho. And like Iceberg Slim said: "Any pimp that believes a whore loves him shouldn't never have fell out of his mommy ass!"

Playboy and me treated him to breakfast on 10th Ave, and I paid his transfer back to Philly. Playboy gave him a bag of weed to help him relax. I gave him a T-shirt and drove him to Newark Penn Station.

His Bitch stayed in Paterson for a while until her pimp got locked up.

Last time I talked to Philly Bob he was working as a salesman in a clothing store. I heard they were back together but that was just what I heard. I hope this story can teach someone a lesson. PIMPIN' AIN'T EASY...and there are good times and there are hard times. Maybe Philly Bob should've joined a rap group because he was a helluva hype man. He could have given Flavor Flav a run for his money. I hope if he ever reads this book he won't get upset about it. And, if so, he's still my man 50 Grand (Philly Bob).

CHAPTER 9

SEVEN LAKES

FIRST I WOULD LIKE to say this is a story that I put a lot of thought into writing. I had to dig deep into my mind and soul and seesaw with my conscience and my inner-self realization. I had to know would this story BUILD or DESTROY. I'll have to leave that to the reader. But one thing I do know is the POWER is the TRUTH and the TRUTH is the POWER. And KNOWLEDGE is something gained from actual experiences. So I decided this story must be told so that knowledge, wisdom, and understanding which is the best part can be learned from my story. I have never told anyone this story before and it is 100% true as I remember.

My father would often take my brother, me, and kids from the neighborhood fishing. My father with his southern roots loved to fish. If he didn't work seven days a week he would have fished everyday from sunup to sundown. My father had taught me to fish at a very young age of about three or four. I loved fishing too. I loved watching my father fish. It seemed as if he was born to be a fisherman. He knew everything about fishing. When the water was too high or too low for fish to bite. Which bait to use and when to use it. He taught me how deep to fish. He taught me how far to cast out. He taught me how to remove certain fish from the hook so they couldn't cut you with their fins. He showed me how to slide the hook gently through the worm's body leaving just enough to dangle underwater to attract a fish's attention. He would come home from work and say to me, "Randy, we going fishing in the morning. We're leaving at 5 A.M., and I mean 5, not a minute after." He would say, "It's a full moon, fish gonna be biting early." Once I heard "fishing" nothing else mattered in the world. I would get my mother's flashlight and stay up until 12 midnight. Then I would go out in all that darkness with a shovel and dig up as many night crawlers as possible. Man, those worms were so big to me. I would be out in the garden with a shovel, flashlight, and a mayo jar. Often I would catch my mother or father or both peeking out of the window smiling at me. But I always pretended not to see them. I had a job to do. Once the jar was full I would punch holes in the top, clean it off, and place it in the refrigerator. The cold from the icebox kept them fresh and alive.

My mother always hated when my father kept his

worms in the icebox. "Daddy, Daddy," I would say. "What Randy," he replied. I said, "I got the worms. They in the icebox." and he'd respond, "Okay, wash up and go to bed. We are leaving early in the morning." So I'd wash my hands, say my prayers, and jump my six-year-old self in the bed. That night I prayed to catch a big fish.

When my father called my name in the morning I jumped out of bed. My mother was packing sandwiches and snacks for us. My father told me to go next-door because Kola (a boy about 16 years old) was going with us. Kola's family had lived there for years. Kola was my brother, WJJ's friend. Kola had brothers and sisters too. His family, like mine, had moved to the eastside of Paterson in hopes of better schooling and a better neighborhood. We loaded up my father's Cadillac Eldorado—all three of us in the front with me in the middle, and we took off.

The ride to Seven Lakes always seemed to take forever. But my father made it fun by telling jokes, farting, and acting like Uncle Remus and Bare Rabbit. Once we arrived there my father would always let me jump on his lap and steer into the park. At least I thought I was steering, but his hands never left the steering wheel and he guided the car into the park. I didn't care. I was driving to me. This all took place long before my mother's Jehovah Witness cult destroyed my childhood and before my brother, Silky poisoned my brain with pimping. At six years old my father was my idol and king of the world. At six years old I was a boy who loved his dad and fishing. That day God heard my prayers I caught the biggest fish! We all caught lots of fish. It was a great day for fishing just like my dad said.

It was getting late and the sun was going down and my father told Kola and me to start packing up, while we packed my father was trying to catch one more fish. It was always hard to get him to quit unless we had no more worms or they just weren't biting or everyone was complaining to leave, starving or bit the hell up with mosquito bites. As Kola and I carried the last of the fishing poles and supplies to the car, Kola told my father that we would be waiting in the car for him.

The next event would haunt me off and on for the next 40 years.

While waiting in the car Kola started asking me strange questions about my penis. Does it get hard? Is it big? How does it look? (Now remember I'm six years old and he's laughing while he's asking me these questions and I'm laughing too.) Then, out of nowhere, he pulls his penis out and starts jerking it. And he tried to get me to touch it. (Now I'm not laughing anymore.) He tried to grab my hand and force it on his penis. He was saying over and over, "Touch it, lick it, squeeze it," and then everything went blank in my mind. (I swear on a stack of Bibles and all of my kids' lives. I can't remember nothing else but my father coming to the car, the ride back home...nothing else comes to me.) NOTHING! Sometimes I wonder if it was a dream. I've heard of people blocking out bad memories. Erasing those traumatic experiences from their minds. And I know for a fact that it was true, because off and on for the last 40 years I've often wondered why I can't remember saying "no" or saying "yes". I'm not even sure it happened but it must've. Why didn't I tell my father? He would've killed him with his bare hands right there on the spot. Why didn't I tell my mother when I got home? It was and still is and I guess will always be a mystery to me.

I remember his family moved that year. And I heard that Kola went to prison. Maybe 20 years later, I would pull up in my parents driveway, walked in the backdoor, and there sitting at the kitchen table with my parents was Kola. I had waited years to ask him about that day. My parents said, "Randy, you remember Kola, right?" When I turned he extended his hand out and I walked right by him and said, "Yes, I remember him, but I have to wash my hands real quick." I ran out the front door and opened my trunk and snatched my pistol out. I ran back in and went into the bathroom. I was sweating like a sick dope fiend. As I threw water on my face over and over I stopped and stared in the mirror. And then it happened, I drifted back 40 years ago to Seven Lakes and Kola in the car. I was reliving the whole scene in my mind while gazing in the mirror. I was lost in thought for what seemed like hours. When I heard my mother calling me, "Ran, Ran." I snapped back to reality. I threw water on my face one more time, and towel it off, and walked out the bathroom with the pistol tucked in the side of my pants. I sat down at the kitchen table with my parents and Kola. He asked me how I was doing. I nodded my head up and down as if to say fine and then I asked him how he was doing. He had just done a long prison bid and was living in a shelter in Paterson. My father told him I was wasting my life away pimping and with all the education I had I wanted to be a pimp. I was thinking if I pulled out my gun and shot him in the head which way would his head fall. Would it fall backwards or would it fall forwards onto my mother's kitchen table. Would blood splatter all over my parents face. I was staring bloody murder at him, when my mother broke the trance and asked me was I all right. I had my right hand under the table. I was rubbing the pistol handle with my fingers when Kola stood up and said, "I have to be getting back to the shelter to beat the curfew." I stood up; I had one last chance to blow his head off. Seconds seemed like minutes, minutes seemed like hours. I've never felt like I felt at that moment again in my life. Then he looked at me and said, "I did a lot of stupid things in my life. But now I am serving God and my life belongs to Jesus." He told me if I wanted I could come to his church with him Sunday. And just like that he was gone. And so were my chances of ever finding out what happened—or ever evening up the score by putting a bullet in his head. And I've never seen him again to this day. And I don't want to.

One day I heard he was as crack head living in the streets of Paterson. Was that his justice? Was that his penalty? Why can't I remember? Was it just a dream? Did it really happen? Should I have shot him or pistol-whipped him? Well, I guess God will have the last word in this.

Dear PARENTS,
Never trust anybody with your children. Never think that kids are safe from the filth and evil in this world because

of good religion. Whenever in doubt remember my trip to Seven Lakes.

CHAPTER 10

COUSIN, DON'T DO IT!

IT WAS A WARM SUMMER night. I had been out to dinner at Red Lobster with my ladies. I would often take them to dinner at different nice places to break the tension of day-to-day grinding. Grinding in those GO-GO Bars with drunk, bad breath men. Getting jean burns on their ass from lap dancing all night for their Daddy. Listening to the small bullshit night after night from lonely men, bored husbands, sex addicts, rapist, perverts, and just men addicted to the GO-GO World. There were some men who'd tip a stripper all night and all she had to do was listen to him talk about his worthless life. How his wife won't fuck him, won't cook, won't clean, won't suck his dick, won't let him fuck her in the ass, won't work, and so on and so forth.

So anyway, I would often take my ladies out to the amusement park, movies, or bars or I would let them take one of my cars and go out bar hopping enjoying themselves. Strange as it may seem I had been taking ladies to work at bars for the last 15 years. I could count on one hand the times I'd been in a GO-GO Bar. I might pop up once in a blue moon to show my face or to let them know that I would pop up. But the bar scene was just not for me.

Anyway, we had just got home and I was so stuffed all I wanted to do was smoke some weed and go to sleep. The faster I went to sleep the quicker I wouldn't have to deal with the ladies in the living room ready to keep the night going. They probably would be up all night smoking and drinking. And probably scheming on all of them jumping into bed with me stoned out of their minds, sucking and fucking me until I felt and looked like a prune.

I had been sleep maybe 45 minutes when my phone starting ringing over and over again. As I fumbled to answer it, I was ready to curse out some nigga or bitch for calling me back to back to back. "Who da fuck is this?" I yelled into the phone with murder in my voice. "Couz, Couz, hello, who is this?" I said. I couldn't make out what he was saying. In between sobs and sniffling I recognized the voice. It was my cousin Leon from down south. "What's wrong cousin?" I yelled over and over into the phone. My cousin Leon was raised by my grandparents and had been sheltered from a lot of things. He had recently met this girl and like many, many young men had fallen in love with the first taste of pussy he got. We had been hearing rumors of how she had him pussy whipped and had his nose open wide enough to drive a freight train through it. Whenever you get a man with no experience messing around with an experienced woman, ho, or bitch, you got your hands full. He had furnished her trailer with new furniture from door-to-door. He had bought her a new car and was making the payments on it. He was going bankrupt and working his self to death. And she in return was partying and living high on the hog. And in return she was fucking everything that moved.

On a previous occasion he had called me while outside a hotel room, he had followed her and a man too. I had talked him into going home. It wasn't worth it to get involved and troubled over a bitch! Especially a worthless bitch that had nothing to offer him but PUSSY!

Anyway, when I finally made out what he was saying I couldn't believe it. He was outside their trailer with a 5-gallon can of gasoline and a match. Inside the trailer he could see his woman through the window fucking and sucking another man dry. Here my cousin was a grown man who was madly in love with the first piece of pussy he touched. And now after everything she had put him through in a year's time he was at his breaking point that everyone reaches sometime in their life. He was calling me crying like a baby with a can of gasoline and a match outside their window watching his beloved hoe ass woman fuck and suck another man's brains out. I was erect in bed and trying to figure out the right things to say for a situation like that.

First, I had to defuse the situation. I didn't want to add fuel to the fire...(little joke). I said, "Couz, think, think, what you 'bout to do. It ain't worth it. Nothing is worth the electric chair. That's double murder you about to commit. Come up north with me, in three months you'll be having so much fun, tonight will feel like nothing but a bad dream. It ain't worth it to throw your whole life away over nothing. Soon as you get here I'll have you soaking up in so much pussy you won't remember that bitch. The bitches I know fuck and suck so good that bitch you got couldn't carry their douche box home." I was talking so fast. I was trying and hoping I was making sense to him. I told him a bitch like that didn't deserve a man like him. Then I lied. I told him how my first love had done the same thing to me but with my best friend of years. I told him she even married him and had twins. I lied, and told him how I laugh now when I see the bitch, broke and on welfare, and begging for change for coke. Her husband had turned her onto drugs and left her for a younger and prettier woman. I even told him how I ordered one of my hoes to spit in her face one day for payback. Then I said, "Listen Couz, every dog has its day, and what goes around comes around. Karma is a real motherfucker." I noticed that he was calming down so I decided to put the icing on the cake when I told him as soon as he gets up north, I'd teach him how to be a PIMP! I even promised to give him his first whore. I had done it...I saved the day!

My cousin did come to Paterson for two years. He worked good jobs and saved his money. I would let him trick with some of the hottest pussies I knew. I never tried to teach him the PIMP GAME. He loved pussy too much. But I'll always remember that night. I saved my cousin from double murder by arson. And I saved some cum-freak-nigga and a southern-freak-ass-hoe. Well, I guess for that night you could call me: CAPTAIN SAVE A HOE!

CHAPTER 11

JASHON, WHY CAN'T YOU JUS' LET ME LOVE YOU?

WHY CAN'T YOU jus' let me love *you*?
It was words I had been hearing my whole life. The same words over and over. If I did let someone love me would I have to love her back? Would I have to trust her? Could I be in New Jersey and her in Mexico and still trust and believe that another man didn't stand a chance?

HOW can someone give love, if they haven't been given love? Is LOVE real? I mean two people holding hands in matrimony and promising each other before God that they'll be with only each other for the rest of their lives.

Sometimes LOVE can choke you like two hands around your neck. If its one thing I've learned from the PIMP GAME is never trust a HOE. *And* LOVE is definitely out of the picture. But it can and does happen to the best of them. Shit, if you have a pet like a dog or a cat around five years you can even catch feelings for a pet. It's human nature.

I have seen strippers at work in bars playing with dicks and tricking and swearing they love their man at home. I have seen women at office jobs, hospital jobs, and everywhere out in the world and have ongoing relationships with men at work with a husband at home and vice-verse.

SO, where is the LOVE? Where is the TRUST? SO, when women say "can you please let me love you?" I see it as "can you please let me hurt you." But being a PIMP I couldn't make a mistake of falling in love, but *I* did.

For the sake of all the readers I would like to say I'm not trying to change your outlook on love. I'm just giving my point of view on love.

So whenever someone says, "why don't you let me love you," just make sure that person has been given love and shown love because someone cannot give you love, if they have never been given love. I guess that's why some people like myself keep things bottled up inside so tight. And when they are not expressed they turn into rage. And in my case my RAGE propelled my PIMP GAME. And now my PIMP GAME has propelled my writing.

Just as much as love can make you feel good, it can also make you feel bad and hurt. And when it hurts, trust me it hurts. There is nothing worse than a broken heart. So I write with RAGE, with bottled up emotions, with fear of giving or receiving love. All these things go into my writing. Through my writing maybe I can help one person or even maybe, just maybe, one day help myself.

CHAPTER 12

WEAK IN THE KNEES

IT WAS 4:30 A.M., when I opened my eyes. I began to wake up on my own now being that I took my son Pumey to work every morning at 5 A.M. He had been home from jail now since May, and was doing well working everyday since he'd gotten out.

Lying next to me was my new love in my life sleeping like a baby. The rain outside was beating like a drum and my dick was hard as a rock. I struggled out of bed to piss this hard-on away. As I was washing my face and brushing my teeth I thought about how I had began to second-guess this relationship I was in. It was nothing new to me being a Pimp at heart always made me second-guess the self-realization of commitment. I speed dressed and kissed my baby and ran out into the early morning rain. The cold raindrops beat on my head and face with sounds of pitter-patter until I jumped in my baby's car. As I fired up the engine "Weak in the Knees" by SWV blasted from the radio. "I get so weak in the knees, hell, I didn't know what had come over me. Shit, I couldn't explain why your lovin' made me weak, your love is sweet it knocks my ass right off my feet," and then I went into a trance. Damn! Here comes another "vision". I recalled how every time I'd gotten in her car there was nothing but those I love you and miss you and can't live without you songs on. I wondered why when I was right here with her everyday. My mind was racing when my son tried to open the car door and startled me and broke my trance. Man, my mind was flying and so was I in the rain.

When I dropped him off I selected back to the number 5 track, "Loving Makes Me Weak". I think best when I'm alone. I had learned that back when I was 17 living in South Carolina with my brother. I was so bored most of the time I could do nothing but concentrate. And the 5 months I did in the juvenile jail drug rehab helped train my brain. Anyway, it didn't take a rocket scientist to know she was fiendin' for her husband who was incarcerated every chance she got. Even though he had been in jail many years and had several more I knew he would get out one day and where would that leave me? I knew where it would leave me: on the short end of the stick with sucker written all over my face, no matter what.

In the 'hood when a female's ex comes home from prison, she could be living in a 13 bedroom mansion with a pool, a two car garage, washer and dryer, and a dishwasher, and sleeping on silk sheets in a heart-shaped waterbed. Trust me, she's gonna sneak away from her new man and 85% of the time get some of that jail dick from her ex. On too many occasions, she had brought up her ex's name to me while we lay in bed. I took off a chain she had bought me. I knew by taking off that chain that I was breaking off this relationship. As the tears poured down my face more and more with "Weak in the Knees" still playing. I wondered why I could never really have or know real love.

Here I was 46 years old and still without trust for the opposite sex. Was I afraid of commitment (as I'd previously questioned)? Was I afraid of failure? Was I just afraid of love?

My Jehovah Witness childhood and that damn pimping had really screwed my brain around. I knew by cutting this off I would cause major pain to my baby, but not as much pain as I would've received by building a future with someone for years and losing it all once the love of her life came home from prison. The "vision" was clear. My mind was made up. I guessed I'm never going to know or feel or have love. Pimping must be my future and destiny.

Baby-Doll was still calling me at least 10 times a day. She would tell me over and over how she wanted me back on any terms. Damn, I wished her new man Elmer J. Fudd could hear this bitch beggin' for me back. She had really only used him to keep her mind occupied until she could get over me. Even though I had pimped on her for 4½ years filled with trips and good times. If Elmer J. Fudd thought keeping her in the house and keeping his dick in her mouth and ass was exciting her he was far from smart.

I guessed pimping was the crutch I used whenever everything else I tried seemed gloomy. They say Pimps are born. If so I guessed God sure dealt me one of the bottom.

It was still raining and in a strange way I felt like God was telling me something. I felt like He was saying, "Jashon, just keep raining down on whoever and whatever you choose."

CHAPTER 13

FATHER, CAN YOU HEAR ME

THEY SAY YOUR parents mess up the first part of your life. And your kids mess up the rest of your life. Those were words I repeated over and over in my mind during my life. Sometimes I would lie in bed paralyzed with pain. But most of the time I would feel like my life was an ongoing fairy tale.

This particular day I was daydreaming about the time I broke into a house with "Black Jesus" and a couple other brothers. As we rummage through the house brothers grabbing jewelry, money, and stereo equipment. I still remember how I was so young and stupid all I took was a red light bulb out the lamp. I laugh to myself as I recall it. Then I would drift back to earlier times in my life at baseball practice. I must've been about 11 years old. I had asked my father for a new glove several times with the new season approaching. At practice I noticed my good friend with a new glove. He was from a single parent home. I knew if he had one I should have one with both of my parents at home. His mother was very young and gorgeous too. But in those days in a single parent household it was tough. And he had four brothers and sisters. I said to him, "Larry, where did you get the new glove?" He said, "Your father bought it for me." I was crippled and numb with pain. It didn't take a rocket scientist to figure out how and why my dad had bought him the glove. As fine as his mother was he should've gotten a glove, batting glove and cleats, wristband, and whatever else he wanted.

The more I turn it seemed my past always turns with me. The more I run, the more my past runs behind me. I wanted to call this book, "Tales of the Paterson Pimp." But the word *tales* sounded too much like I would be telling lies. And I have too much respect for myself and my work as an author to ever lie to my readers. I write from my soul. And I continue to work on my soul every day because: *My Soul is Still PIMPIN'*.

CHAPTER 14

TWO HUNDRED POUNDS

ME AND PLAYBOY were at the Triangle Go-Go Bar in the Bronx in the Hunt's Point section. It was BBW Night (Big Beautiful Women) was stripping tonight. We had our Big Bitches with us. The only problem was all dancers had to be 200 pounds and over. My bitch was about 170 pounds and Playboy's bitch was about 180 pounds. We thought since we had a special invite from Rambo, the promoter, we thought the weight wouldn't be a problem. It was just a couple of pounds, we thought.

As soon as we approached the door the security team stopped us. Even though the bitches were looking hot that night, if they weren't 200 pounds and over they couldn't get in. As we debated at the door with them over pounds and weight Rambo came out with a scale. They actually had bitches outside standing on scales to make sure they were 200 pounds and over and not a pound under.

Being that we had traveled from Jersey over there they let the bitches in to work as long as we paid double for them to get in.

We did pay and at least my bitch made my money back. But the bitch Playboy brought turned out to be a Big Fat Funky Zero. She didn't even make the tip in back.

I told my man Playboy I would tell this story because we still remember the night they had bitches getting weighed in to go strip. You know what they say it's more cushion for the pushin'. And if you never been to a BBW Strip Show, you gotta see one. Those Big girls really do their thing. I respect them to the fullest. And they draw large crowds all the time. I once heard a player say, "There's nothing a skinny girl can do for me, but show me where a big girl is at!

And that *player* might have been me!!!!

CHAPTER 15

IF HE ONLY KNEW...

9:40 P.M. I was sitting home. Wet-Wet just called and told me my daughter needed her swimsuit and Hannah Montana bag she left with me when I had her and Arionna (my other daughter) for the weekend. She told me her man was on the way over and not to come yet. *For some reason she doesn't want me to meet him,* I thought to myself. Baby-Doll had been calling and texting me all day. We went to lunch today and she let me know for the hundredth time how she wanted me back. How she missed dancing and how bored to death she was with Elmer J. Fudd. The nigga really thought he had stolen something from me. If he only knew she was laying in his bed calling me over and over again. For the last six months, Elmer J. Fudd had made her his personal sex slave...more like built in young pussy. If only he knew how much money he had cost me. In six months she could've made me well over $50,000 dancing and here she was laying in Elmer J. Fudd's bed sucking and fucking his ugly fat ass dry. Was I upset? A little. Was I jealous? Hell no! I had taught her everything she knows.

WET-WET's man had come home from jail about 2 or 3 months ago and rushed to get her pregnant. He even bought her an engagement ring. I guess she had spun her magic web around him like she had done to me. My only concern was that he was so pussy whipped that if I'd come within 50 feet of that house he might've shot me on sight to keep me from being around WET-WET.

Sometimes pussy can make men do strange and stupid things.

It's 10:00 P.M. and Baby-Doll just sent me her last text for the night. I guess Elmer J. Fudd got off work at 10:00. Earlier she had asked me could we meet up after he went to work at 2:00 P.M.

Imagine Elmer J. Fudd about to come home to a young fat yellow ass that Baby-Doll had and all day long she had been calling the PATERSON PIMP. Or imagine me dropping off a bag to my daughter with WET-WET inside her apartment with her man and she couldn't even come out to say hello. These were just a few of life experiences in my life. But I called them "best experiences" because I'm alive and here writing. Armed and dangerous—I'm armed with a pen and paper.

CHAPTER 16

TO WHOM IT MAY CONCERN:

IT WAS THE NIGHT before Baby-Doll was supposed to receive her settlement of $13, 709.23. It was her settlement for injuries sustained in a car accident we had been in April 12, 2008. I was still feeling mortified at the fact she had promised to give me half. I knew that the end represents the means, no matter what sacrifice. I was going to make sure once I got that money in my hand her grieving would not be an overnight process. Well, in case you're confused let me explain what the hell I'm talking about.

If you've read my first book *The Paterson Pimp*, you would know I held Baby-Doll down for four and a half years. She was my bottom woman with me in my forties and her in her twenties. That was great pimping for a man my age, nowadays; it had not been all peaches and cream, 'cause pimping ain't easy. She was definitely a moneymaker. She worked in the bars every night like her life depended on it. I had sure turned her into a real down bitch! And once she understood that pussy was powerful there was no stopping her. Here was a hoe that loved paying her man. I had read one time a pimp was only promised 2 or 3 good bottom women in his life. Baby-Doll was the third and probably my last. There had been La'Pue in the late 80s, Miss AC in the 90s, and now Baby-Doll in the 2000. It was funny that they all were high yellow. All three of their mothers were addicts. Only Baby-Doll had a real father figure growing up. They all had left home early trying to grow up fast. Most of the time that's how young girls meet pimps likes me. Pimps who appear to be sheep's, but really were like dangerous wolves in disguise.

Anyway, March 21, 2009, at 7:30 a.m., Baby-Doll had crashed my Caddy. I loved that car. It was in mint condition, too. I had given her the keys to go to her apartment to pick something up. She only lived 5 minutes away. She had to be at work at 8:00 a.m. She left my house about 7:20 and 7:30 she called me crying. She had run head-on with a 70,000-pound garbage truck.

Now here was where the story began.

February 22, 2009, Baby-Doll had been hired back at the same McDonald's she was at when I met her. If you remember from the first book, I had told her she could retire after 5 years. Well, I held her down for 4 and a half and she only had 6 more months. We had a 5-year plan to hustle hard for 5 years with her dancing and me giving parties (bachelor) and then we would retire from the game.

Here was where everything got tricky. After she crashed my car, I noticed she was acting strange. Strange in a way that only a PIMP knows something was going on. I didn't know if it was another PIMP. Everyday my mind was racing. I knew once she started working that square bitches would start filling her head with bullshit. "Girl, you don't need him!", "Girl, you don't have to strip no more." She was only dancing on the weekends now anyway. My father had told me a long time ago that once a woman got a car, a job, and a telephone, a man was in for trouble. And man was he right. She was acting more and more stranger everyday. All of my life I had this sixth sense. On many occasions, I could be home asleep and wake up with a certain feeling and go to a bar and catch one of my hoe's doing something wrong. Or go to someone's house I was dating and catch them cheating. That had happened many times in my life.

Well, one early morning, I woke up about 4 a.m., in April with that same feeling. I jumped up, took a shower, and decided to drive down to Baby-Doll's house. I had that feeling but I doubted she was up to no good. What the fuck! I figured since I had the key to her apartment I would wake her up and give her some morning dick. I loved to fuck in the morning. If you're a man, you know what I'm talking about. My dick was always it's hardest in the morning. As I rode down the street there were no cars on the block. I passed a black car with silver chrome on it. It was double parked one block before her block. It was a girl getting out. As I passed it I thought to myself, *Some nigga is dropping a bitch off after a long night of fucking.* As I stopped on Baby-Doll's block I was directly across from her house. I noticed someone walking up the street. The closer they got the more they looked familiar. Then it hit me, oh shit, it's Baby-Doll! I jumped out of my car and said, "Come here, come here!" She started crying and was trying to open her gate. I pushed the gate closed and asked her where was she coming from. Like I didn't know. Well, I didn't know. Was it another pimp? Was it a trick? Was she making money behind my back? Was it a dyke? Or did she have a lesbian licking her pussy all night? Somehow, I persuaded her to get in my car with me after I promised her I wouldn't hit her. Now being a *pimp* I had to be careful. I didn't want to come off like a hurt boyfriend or husband so I played the "tell them what their itching to hear routine". I needed to get information. I had a reputation to uphold. My reputation always meant a lot to me. After about a hour she told me it was a guy named Henry, who worked at welfare. She claimed she had met him when he came to the Drive-thru window at her job. The story was a little farfetched but that's all I had to go on.

If it was just a nigga she wanted to fuck, I had no problem with a bitch sneaking out for some dick at night. Shit, I was by no means an angel myself. Well, Pimp's don't cheat; we have the best of both worlds. Pussy and women come in abundance for players. This was why they say, "Pimping ain't easy." This could be the tragic side of pimping. I had to stay focused from this moment on, not like I wasn't, but this was new for me with Baby-Doll. She had always been a real 100% dedicated bottom woman.

Anyway, I took the bitch back home after an hour of quizzing her. I called Wet-Wet on the phone. As soon as she heard my voice she said, "What's wrong?" Over the years Wet-Wet would always know when something was wrong as soon as she heard my voice. One thing I could say about Wet-Wet was that we couldn't get along for nothing in the world. We had argued and fought like cats and dogs. Well, we argued because I stopping hitting her a long time ago when she told me one night, "You hit me for the last time," and jumped on my ass. I knew right then, I would never hit her again. Wet-Wet might of hurt my ass in my sleep or something.

Well, anyway, I told her I needed to talk. She told me to come over and she'd let me talk her ears off. I always believed where else do you go for answers about a woman, but to another woman. After she gave me her input and helped me with my hemorrhoid cream, I went and lay down in my daughter Jada's room with her and went to sleep.

When I woke up I kissed my daughter and gave her a big hug. I knocked on Wet-Wet's bedroom door and thanked her for her time and left. WET-WET had always been there for me when I needed her. She was there for me when one of my daughter's was molested. Whenever I was in trouble with the law. Whenever I was drunk out of my mind or whatever the situation she was always there to lend an open ear. Wet-Wet's pregnant right now and I wish her nothing but the best. When I left her house I felt that we were closer now than when we used to be. We used to be like gasoline and fire.

I decided to ride through the McDonald's Drive-thru and check on Baby-Doll. It had been less than 5 hours since I caught her creeping in the early morning hours. As I approached the window I spotted her first, she was laughing and joking with her co-workers. Damn, she was in a good mood for a woman who just got caught creeping less than 5 hours ago. She never even recognized my voice on the intercom when I placed my order. When she saw me she had a look on her face like I had shit on my forehead. I said, "Having fun, uh, baby." She said, "I'm not having fun." When I got my food I pulled out and made a left, my head jerked to the left into the parking lot. Damn! It was a black car with silver chrome on it like the one I saw her get out of that morning. My mind was trying to rewind to when I passed it. I said over and over that that looks like the same car. That car in the parking lot belongs to a co-worker in there. I called him Elmer J. Fudd or maybe Mr. Magoo. I made a note in my brain to keep my eyes open. If Elmer J. Fudd was fucking with my hoe, he was fucking with my doe! To be continued...

CHAPTER 17

ON YOUR MARK, GET SET, (HO) GO!

IT WAS 2 DAYS before my birthday. Baby-Doll was really starting to annoy me by calling me all day. I guess Elmer J. Fudd was boring the fuck outta her. I had bought a Lexus ES 300 with the money she gave me. She had been telling me lately how she missed the sporty life of fast money, fast cars, and all the excitement that goes along with the "PIMP and HO" game.

Everyday I wonder if Elmer J. Fudd (her new boyfriend) with the black car with silver chrome around it knew what a Boss Bottom Bitch he had. But he was a trick and tricks only think with one head. And it ain't the head on their shoulders. Mr. Fudd was sleeping in the bed with thousands of dollars and didn't even know it. Baby-Doll would laugh and tell me how he would fall off of her sweating and out of breath after he'd cum. She would say she would lay there sexually frustrated. Now I know you're wondering why I'm hating on Elmer. I don't really know him, but as far as I'm concern he's guilty by association!

Baby-Doll was the star that Jashon built. Now she was working at McDonald's and Burger King. I even started hearing rumors in the street of how she wanted me back. The lure of the money was strong. But to go against my rules and compromise my principles could be dejavu. Or even worse next time she got rabbit in her blood. It might cost me my life.

Baby-Doll had been out of the game about six months now. And no doubt she was lost and heartbroken without her Daddy Jashon. For 4½ years I kept her humping but we damn sure lived ghetto fabulous. Now she was wasting her life making Ronald McDonald rich and keeping Elmer J. Fudd's dick wet. I would have to make a decision quick. It won't be long before she quits and gives up on the square world. Pussy is power and she knows that! I laughed inside when she showed me Elmer J. Fudd house key. I thought 25 years ago I would have taken that key and he would have come home to nothing but the tacks in the wall. Yes, Baby-Doll was approaching the finish line. It's time to HO up!

I had another big problem... and her name was MITSY BISHI BABY.

Misty was not a stripper or a prostitute. She was a beautiful, sexy, intelligent independent Black queen. And she treated me like a king. Now Mitsy Bishi Baby and I had a history. I had met her back in the early 90s and fell hard for her. But I was married and never told her. When she found out it was too late. She was 21 and in love. I never told her about my previous pimping. All she knew or thought was that I was a hard working Black man. Our feelings for each other would reach the sky.

What I am about to share is about one of the most mature things I'd ever done in life. We came together and made a decision with me being married and her wanting more out of life (we loved each other so much) that we would let each other go. But we planned one more date, which was a concert at Madison Square Garden in New York. We hopped on a bus. Knowing it was our last time seeing each other made the concert one big blur. To this day, we can't remember who performed that night. And as we rode back to Jersey on the bus we sat nose to nose, lips to lips all the way home.

Knowing in our minds that it would be our last time together, but knowing in our hearts that we both had lost a part of our souls...we would never get it back.

I knew when I kissed her lips it was for the last time and when I stepped off that bus (on my way home) that I had just stepped away from one of the best things that had ever happen to me in my life.

Now, here it was 17 years later and Mitsy Bishi Baby

was once again back in my life, in more ways than one. She *is* the only thing between me going back to the PIMP GAME.

Mitsy Bishi Baby is so good to me that I don't even know why everyday I consider going back to pimping. She doesn't know the struggles I have with myself: day and night when I lay beside her. She gives me confidence to keep writing and strengthens me because she believes in me. Mitsy Bishi Baby is the first woman to ever get me open without using her pussy or her mouth.

As I write this book I ponder my situation. Will I go back to Baby-Doll and the PIMP GAME, lots of money, late nights, resting and dressing...or will it be the square life with Mitsy Bishi Baby? On your mark, get set, (HO) go!

CHAPTER 18

HAPPY BIRTHDAY, ME

IT WAS SEPTEMBER 17th 3:30 in the morning. It's my birthday. There I was again waking up alone in my bed on my birthday. I fell asleep at 8:30 p.m., and woke up at 1:30 a.m. When 12 o'clock struck and my birthday came in I was asleep. I rushed to look at my phone to see who really cared, who had called or who had texted me at the strike of 12 when my birthday came in. My phone had gone dead so I couldn't check any missed calls. I would have to wait, but I could check my text messages.

There was one from Toya, who I had met several years ago. She was walking home in the pouring rain and I had stopped and offered her a ride. Her and her man had a quarrel and she had left his house and there she was walking in the pouring rain like she was walking in between the raindrops.

There was another text from Baby-Doll, she no doubt had snuck out of bed with Elmer J. Fudd and probably quietly texted me from the bathroom to say, "HAPPY BIRTHDAY DADDY. I MISS YOU AND LOVE YOU." She probably wanted to say come rescue me from this boring and pathetic life I'm living with Mr. Fudd.

The other text came from Wet-Wet and my daughter

Jada. It read: "Happy 25th Birthday! Lol. We love you." WET-WET had a man now. But Mike Tyson and Hurricane Katrina put together couldn't have stopped her from letting my daughter wish me Happy Birthday at 12 o'clock. Did she sneak out of bed like Baby-Doll? If I was a betting man I'll say she didn't hide a thing.

The next text was from Cortney. Now Cortney was someone I met many years ago when she would come to Jersey from New York for the summer. Our summer nights would be filled with fun and excitement. She was young and lied about her age. And I guessed I lied about being married. But our friendship has stood through the test of time. She means a lot to me and always will. But when she got older she had a beautiful daughter by one of my partners from 17th Ave. who also later in life turned into one of my Pimp Buddies. He was the one who summoned me to White Castle to let me know Baby-Doll's ex boyfriend was out to kill me. And to be careful and I'll never forget him for that. It put me on alert and probably helped save my life. And for that he'll always be my mellow fellow. But as far as Cortney, she was and always will be special to me. And having a daughter by my man from 17th Ave will always keep me from thinking about a serious relationship with her.

And then, the next text was from my Mitsy Bishi Baby. Her text read: "HAPPY BIRTHDAY! I LOVE U. CALL ME SOON AS U GET THIS TEXT. I DON'T CARE WHAT TIME IT IS."

She was really doing her best to lock me down. We had met back in the early 90s and began a relationship filled with promise and possibilities. And after more than 15 years had began a phone relationship that just kept growing and growing. And here we were now privately dating. I say privately because I had been pimping for the last 14 years and she had a husband who had been in prison many years and still had many to go. We decided to stay on the low for a while until we decided to take it to another level. And believe it or not we began talking again after she had purchased and read my first book, *The Paterson Pimp*. Here was a woman who had read my life story of pimping women and drug dealing and drug abuse. She read my book and still wanted me. Now that was what I respected and admired about her. She was rare and unique and that made her special to me. I guessed maybe somewhere down the line she had experienced some kind of pain like me. And together maybe we could bring each other joy and happiness.

For many years as a child I was hurt on my birthdays. Growing up in that Jehovah Witness cult didn't allow me to celebrate it. I would lay and pray sometimes for a birthday cake. I just wanted a cake with my name on it. La'Pue was my first women in the PIMP GAME to buy me a birthday cake. I can't remember how old I was but I cried like a baby inside, of course. Well, maybe a little on the outside too. I also cried at one of my jobs when a white girl asked me to help her decorate a X-mas tree. I had never done that before. Being a Jehovah Witness prevented us from celebrating X-mas too. A feeling came over me I couldn't explain I guessed it was the spirit of X-mas. When I was young my X-mas was when my mother finally said I could go next-door to (RC) aka Shareem Black Jesus' house. His family went all out for X-mas. When I walked into his house it was like stepping in a Toys 'R' Us store. They had everything in there. His brothers, Wayne, Floyd, and sister Cerese (R.I.P) had it all. Me and (RC) were like brothers. We were the same age. We had the same babysitter. Went to the same nursery, camps, and even the same grade school and high school. When most kids were picky and strict about their toys, RC's joy was in seeing my joy in playing with his X-mas gifts. I could touch or play with anything it didn't matter to him. You don't find many kids or friends like that. And I've never forgotten him for that. And this went on for all of our childhood years. When we were about 8 years old, we cut our hands with a knife and rubbed our blood together and became Blood Brothers for life.

Well, it's about 5:30 a.m., and I'm getting sleepy. It's my birthday today and thank God he allowed me to live to see another one. I'll call MITSY BISHI BABY when I wake up. Oh yeah, I am 46 years old this day.

HAPPY BIRTHDAY! RANDY JACKSON a.k.a "JASHON" THE AUTHOR OF THE PATERSON PIMP. The first brother to give a Lock Door GO-GO Party in Paterson and the first street hustler from Paterson to write a book about it.

HAPPY BIRTHDAY TO ME!

JASHON (ANTHONY J. HUSKEY): my oldest son Jonathan's younger brother wrote this story. When he sent it to me I knew I had to put it into print so I would like to thank him and wish him the best. Keep writing Anthony because you have talent and the world needs to know it. Peace.

WESTSIDE PARK

Written by: Anthony J. Huskey

Paterson, New Jersey
3:00 P.M.

THERE WERE SCREAMS heard all around Jamarcus as he lay face down in a pool of blood near the concession stand in Westside Park. A woman standing next to him dropped her ice cream cone, and bent down to snatch up her kid. She took off into the other direction, nearly vomiting as she ran for safety. Someone yelled for help at the sight of all the dark blood, combat boots of the park's security could be heard running toward them.

There was a cry from a familiar voice nearby, and

although Jamarcus was badly hurt, he identified the calls of his name to be Kayla, his fiancée. He tried to rollover, but couldn't. He was too weak and immobile.

Park security reached Jamarcus, and they rolled him onto his back. More shrills rang out at the sight of his wounds.

He looked to his right and that's when he saw Kayla and their daughter, Jakiya, standing amongst the crowd of soccer players, who he'd previously been watching during a sunny afternoon game, right before they'd been called to a half.

There were sirens heard in the distance.

Jamarcus' eyes roamed the crowd for his attacker, before he settled his gaze on Kayla. He blinked and she faded from his vision.

Oh, no!

Snatching his eyes open, he tried to speak, but his lids closed again.

The paramedics scrambled around him and began to work on the young man before them.

Time seemed to freeze for Jamarcus. He was suddenly forgetting why he was even at the park. He had a flashback, a memory of him and his twin sister, Lilian, playing in the exact same park when they were children flashed through his mind. He saw Lilian take a headfirst dive down a ten-foot slide, only to be caught by their now deceased mother, Viola, at the bottom. Realizing that he was standing on the merry-go-round, he spun himself, building up the momentum of the large play-toy. Faster and faster he went, dizzying himself, and that's when he heard his mother's voice warning him to slow down. It was too late, though. He staggered and lost his balance. He tried to catch himself, but the fall was inevitable. Lashing out his arm as he flipped over the railing to meet the ground, the cracking of bones could be heard fifteen feet away, as Viola frantically made her way over to her baby boy. Just as she knelt down to check on him, everything went black, and Jamarcus slipped into darkness.

***

"Hey, you!" the cops yelled at a hooded Chavis, as he ran through the mass of people in Westside Park, cuffing the hunting knife he'd just seconds before gutted Jamarcus with.

"Stop!" someone shouted.

"Shit!," he exclaimed, seeing the black uniforms of park security twenty yards in front of him, headed into his direction. He had to do something, and fast.

The people around him were no longer in a frenzy over Jamarcus' stabbing, and they now stood staring, wondering why he was running, and who the police and park security were chasing.

Approaching a larger crowd of people, he pulled out a nine-millimeter Beretta and fired a shot into the air. In a panic, people began to scurry in every which direction, shielding him from his pursuer's view. Just to be certain that he'd caused enough distraction, he spotted a young Hispanic woman pushing a stroller, and approaching her swiftly, he slashed the back of her thigh with the hunting knife, and without thought, gave the stroller a shove and sent it hurdling over.

"Ah," the woman cried from the ground cradling her thigh, "My baby!" she screamed echoes of hysteria.

The sound of combat boots was getting closer. He took a sharp left and ducked behind a tree. The police and security stopped to assist the screaming woman and her baby.

Chavis smiled.

He removed his hoodie, pulling it over his shoulders. Turning his back to the melee of pedestrians and government officials, he made his way over to the black and gray Kawasaki motorcycle he'd ridden on. Mounting the sporty crotch rocket, he tucked the nine millimeter safely into his waistband, wrapped the bloodied blade into his soon to be discarded hoodie and secured it in a compartment under his seat, for the time being, then revved up the engine of his stolen getaway vehicle, without being noticed sped off having accomplished what he'd set out to do that tragic night of his bosses murder... kill Jamarcus.

JASHON (YOUNG LOVE): This is an email from a close friend of mine from so long ago. She begged me not to print it, but I had to because I've received many letters in my life, but this one is the realest I've ever received.

E-MAIL
1/11/09

I waited a long time for this moment!!!!
If I can recall and when it comes to you I have very clear memories of you and I!! You simply walked away you wrote a book about it! Do you realize that I started seeing other guys because you hurt me so bad and I was so young I couldn't understand? My mother knows who you are only because I cried over you for days she tried to explain

to me that I was too young for love and my time would come when I got older but I couldn't make her understand that being with you matured me and the things we did made me a woman!!! I am 41 years old now and I can remember what the inside of your house looks like (on 31st Street) I can see you and I sharing an intimate moment and me saying to you I'm only 16. Summer of '82, I remember the chain incident!!!! Lol!!!!! I even remember getting it in in your mother's car in the driveway and your father catching us!!!! lmao!!!!! You were everything to me and when I say you made me a beautiful woman you did you molded me at a very young age to want more and to be more. I can't say that about any other man I encountered in my life. I still make sure my bra and panties match 'cause of you!!!! Lol !!!!! You made me sexy I may not have been the prettiest girl in the group but I definitely was the sexiest and I have you to thank for that you gave me the confidence I have today but you also made me very hesitant when it comes to love its 1 of the reasons why I can't maintain a relationship today. I don't blame you but being with you at such a young age set my standards very high because to me you were everything a woman wanted in a man!!!! Being with you physically at such a young age really set the bar high none of them cats matched the intensity and the attraction we shared!!!!!! I'd give anything to feel that way about a man again in this lifetime!!

I will read your book but you will never be the man in that book to me. You will always be my first real love whenever someone asks me if I ever been in love I tell them yeah it was a very long time ago but it always seems like it was just yesterday!!! If I had to write a book about my life you would be chapter 1 because that's when my life started with you!!!!!!!!!!!!!! I did look for the pics I have the one pic of u in a heart frame I knew where that 1 was it was separate from other pics of you eating a slice of pizza on Park Ave but ur dressed with a brim hat all in black and Ya Ya is in that pic but I think coolie or just got the one with you, Preem, Shadee and some other cats all dressed up. My mom said to tell you hi she wanted to know what you looked like I told her u look the same she laughed and said he must still look good!!!! Lol!!! See u on the 28th looking forward to it!!!!!

JASHON (FREDERICK STONE): This letter is from my main man F. Stone. When he first emailed me this notation I was a little upset. Then I came to terms with myself and I understood that when you put your life out there in a book that everyone can and will have an opinion. So I decided to write Frederick back to thank him for taking time out to writer a brother and also check him. When Frederick wrote me back he told me it wasn't anything like that. That he was just speaking his mind and giving his opinion on my book. I told him I would print the letter to let the world see how he "CHECKED" me. I'll always respect my man Frederick Stone. Stay up player and I'll hear from you soon. Peace.

FREDERICK STONE

12-12-08

What's good R.J.?... Fred here... Frederick Stone! You dropped my wife a message in thanks about purchasing your book. I'm incarcerated, and my wife just forwarded your message to me, and I just wanted to take out the time to get back with you. I've already completed the entire book... my opinion on it, I believe you have the skills to become a great writer. There are a few things in the book I became questionable about. Randy, I don't knock no one for how they use the word PIMP, I grew up in South

Central L.A., where Figueroa was one of the biggest strolls, and as a youngster I learned the game from some of the best. And one thing I learned as I begin doing my own things was, only use sex as form of an award. Randy, you was doing your own girls, like a norm, was hooked, and going to it unprotected, and from the impression I got from the book, there was never a stable family, one was jealous of the other, and others were creepin'. There should had never been in any way possible, someone could come alone, but the sex down good on one of my girls, and she give him the key to the apartment. Now Randy, I'm not knocking you, but I would have to call you a MACK, then I would PIMP. A MACK can get a broad to do anything for him, but that doesn't mean he's a PIMP, a PIMP has no love, remorse or sympathy in his heart for a broad, its' all about him money. And I now all this stuff I'm telling you, you already know, but I have already let two other people read it, and they felt the same about the sexing your woman part... So you and Baby doll still together, right? .... Randy, I would definitely like to hear back from you, and I'm going to give you my direct address, so if you like you can get a me directly, however, it's all good. I'm going to see if I can locate your son's book and check that out. Oh!, I heard, well, saw your book in the Assets Magazine, the Premier issue. MY direct address is... Holla at me when you can playa!!!!! Fred.

JASHON (SUPREME DIVINE ALLAH): One day I saw Supreme and I was telling him how I was working on my second book. He suggested that I should write about the 5% Nation being that it played a big part in our lives. I asked him if he would like to do it and he said he would. And here it is in his own words. I know it's a little different from what I write about but everything touches different people in different ways. And I hope this reaches and touches someone too. Thank you, Supreme, and I'll end this with...Peace.

SUPREME DIVINE ALLAH

SUMMARY OF MYSELF

I'm African-American. Born and raised in Paterson, New Jersey. Generally, I grew up in Alabama projects. I'm a realtor investor, a husband and father of two children for the past twenty-seven years. I've been a member of the Nation of Gods and Earths commonly known as The Five Percenters. I don't claim to be active the entire twenty-seven years, however, I have been heavily involved the past twenty years. Perhaps, at this time I've begun to grasp the concept of the Culture and furthermore I desire to make changes in my life, and naturally I wanted to teach everyone I was acquainted with and encounter with through my travels from 1988 up until now. I've taught approximately 80 people and within Paterson, I'm currently teaching a civilization that is geared towards the youth and the primary objective of these teachings is for the improvement of the youth: Common Courtesy for Self and Others, Promoting Education, Moral and Ethics, Character Development, History, and most of all the Doctrines and Concept of the Nation of Gods and Earths. I'm also one of the brother's who helped establish our monthly parliament in Paterson. The parliament were collectively discussed our nation business. I am also responsible for composing our parliament procedures. I'm one of the founders of a Righteous event that is entitled the Day of the Babies. This glorious event takes place annually and has been a success for the past fifteen years. Primarily my role in this function is security in fact I established the security department within this function. Well, basically this is a brief summary about myself in regard to my involvement in the Nation of Gods and Earths.

PASSION FOR MY CULTURE

Now because of my deep concern and passion for my culture I chose to write about the transition that took place in Paterson, in respect to the Nation of Gods and Earths, however, before elaborating the reader must understand my concerns for writing this.

First and foremost, the NGE (Nation of God and Earths) had a tremendous impact on the youth in Paterson, in terms of them becoming conscious. A lot of young people were illiterate. Fortunately, the Grace of the Gods and Earths impacted the youth in such a fashion that they began to take a personal interest in education and consequently develop literacy skills. Furthermore, the NGE helped the youth become critical thinkers as well as how to examine information properly. The Youth also adapt how to eat nutritional and wholesome. The Nation had given them self value, more specific Black pride, and self-esteem. These teachings gave the youth a purpose of life.

The Nation of Gods and Earths made it cool for the young to want to be intelligent and educated. Ironically, before the youth embraced these teachings it was corny to be smart or you were considered a nerd and were afraid to carry books to school. We had even changed our perspectives on how we viewed women. There was a time when we would not allow our women to walk the streets at night by themselves. Such act was forbidden. Brothers had more respect for women those days. They used to address the Black women in a respectful manner. Terms like: queen, earth or sister. Not degrading names like: bitches and hoes. And when a sister had got pregnant we weren't quick to encourage a woman to have an abortion. And there was less division and separation with brothers during this period. Don't get me wrong, there was, is, and always will be diversity and differences in terms of geographical location; however, I assure you it is the truth. I attest to, at time in the history of Paterson, when the Gods (Black men) was traveling to various areas in Paterson to discuss their ideology with all those who shared that common thread of teaching. And a result of this had minimized the violence amongst us during this time.

When Allah's teachings were echoing and flourishing through the city of Paterson, we were more unified. We had more respect for one another. There was a genuine love we had for one another, less confusion, more peace. In fact, we had a favorite saying when two or more individuals had a quarrel or conflict we would say, "Don't be so quick to result to physical violence. First, take it to the mental (communicate) and see if you guys can resolve your differences." We would also say, "The first one who execute violence is a devil and he should be dealt with accordingly." Now in this day in time, I asked myself, what happened? And as I reflected back in history and revisit with images in my mind of how Paterson was once predominately influence by the Gods and Earths, there was a time in the early eighties, more so from 1980 up until 1985 the teachings of our beautiful culture was echoing out through the city of Paterson (land of peace) and expeditiously the youth was gravitating towards our attracting power rapidly. The youth were enrolling in the Nation daily. Me, personally, I refer to it as a righteous epidemic of the early eighties in Paterson. Even the people who did not embrace or accept this way of life were affected by it in some form or fashion. Perhaps, adopting our unique language that our founding father Allah composed from the supreme alphabets. I cannot forget the Gods and Earths peculiar style that was very impressionable to the rest of the youth in their surroundings. The NGE influence was not constricted to our town, this way of life had impacted the world in some form or fashion especially the hip-hop industry. The hip-hop industry was heavily influential by the NGE. The industry became another outlet to convey NGE teachings.

Now just to mention a few more things on how we influenced some of the people of that time, a lot of people were greeting one another by saying peace. This term was also used when people departed form one another. Peace was a terminology we substituted for hello and goodbye. In fact, the Gods and Earths made word semantics popular. For example, we used to say things like: we don't say hello because hell is low and we don't believe because a person can't be and leave at the same time. And for those who know what a Be-boy stance is, we made that popular. A Be-boy stance is when your arms is folded and your right hand is over your left hand symbolizing positive prevail negativity and your feet was positioned. This also symbolized you were standing on your square (truth) according to my understanding; a person should stand on the truth and not lie. And your feet were positioned in a 90-degree angle.

Now as time crept upon us, approximately in 1985, I can recall vividly how ironically crack cocaine were placed in our community (common-unity). It was as though the current of the atmosphere changed swiftly according to my spectacles. This was the beginning of the turning point for the Gods and Earths to relinquish their positive and astonishing magnetic on the community. You began to see a lot of Gods selling and using crack, a lot of Gods and Earths wasn't exercising their lessons like they normally did. The women in our Nation basically reflected and mimicked the men. The women eventually disregarded their refinement, meaning three fourth of clothing despite all this and handful remained steadfast on the square (truth). However, generally the NGE was not building as strong as they once were. The city of Paterson was always infested with drugs; however, there was something about that crack that was overwhelming in terms of causing the city to be dysfunctional in a way I've never attested to. This drug had definitely neutralized the Nation of Gods and Earths. Ironically, these drugs were placed in our community during a time we were becoming conscious and very powerful and these teachings were attracting a lot of youth and the oppressor does not want the youth to wakeup and become aware of their innate abilities because the enemy knows that they will begin to change themselves and their conditions around them. You see, the enemy want us to continue to use drugs, sell drugs, fight and kill one another, disrespecting our women, not being fathers to our children, not pursuing education, and most of all the enemy want the diasporas of the African people all over the planet to remain disunities, therefore, this will allow the enemy to maintain power over us, maintain control over us. You see the enemy success is based on our ignorance, so my beloved brothers and sisters it is far pass the time for us to revitalize, reunite, and start teaching our babies civilization like we used to teach in the early eighties peace. Your brother and companion for freedom, justice, and equality.

Supreme Divine Allah
All praises due to
Allah and the first 9 borns

The PATERSON PIMP

vs.

BARRACUDA BYTCH

IT WAS THE MONTH before my book was to come out. For the last six months I had dedicated my whole well-being to writing and completing my book, *THE PATERSON PIMP*. My brain had been a sponge to any and everything I saw and heard about "how to write and publish your own book." I was determined to finish what I had started. I had sound...the wind, and was ready to let Paterson and the world reap the whirlwind. Many people thought that I shouldn't write about and reveal my pain and experiences of my life and pimping, the obstruction would be not to, but I did it anyway.

A friend of mine who owns an African Book store downtown Paterson, was going to let me put my book in his store when I was done with it. He kept telling me about this female author he wanted me to meet. She had one book out called *Anonymous* and was working on another. He told me she could offer advice on certain areas of self-publishing and writing so I was more than eager to meet her.

Well, one day I decided to go down to the African Book store, and to my amazement she was there. They say first impressions last a lifetime. And they also say never judge a book by its cover.

But here she was, with a low haircut and all. The low cut sent off a sense of strength and quiet dignity. Her bedroom eyes let me know she was very mysterious. Her medium but small frame gave off the notion that she could move gracefully (more than on the dance floor) if she had to. And her "ass" fitted in those jeans like a glove could do more than transform a priest into a pervert. She could have a preacher fornicating at the drop of a dime. Yes, even being a PIMP and knowing the PIMP GAME had nothing to do with sex. She sure could temporarily push me beyond my reasonable bounds.

As I began to talk to her I wanted to pick her brain not only about writing, but also about her. I wanted to know was she really intelligent or was she some pathetic tramp with cleavage all out who probably lost her virginity in the backseat of a Ford Pinto. One thing I do know was that she didn't lack self-esteem and she had a lot of knowledge on how to self-publish my book. She gave me names, and numbers to people who could edit, photograph, and also print my book. Before I left I decided to try her chin and invite her to one of my upcoming GO-GO parties. And even though she wasn't into women, she said that she would think about it. With a woman like herself (even to think about it) was a moral accomplishment.

Within the next month, whenever we saw each other in passing it was always big hellos and good short positive conversation...UNTIL I finished the book. It was at the printer being put together. When I saw her I was excited to tell her that my book was completed. But it was like she had turned into "SYBIL" with another personality. She asked me was I sure it had enough pages and that people she knew and books that she had read who had written autobiographies (had put more time and pages into their works. She was just suggesting...before the printer completed the book.) I knew she had a good point, but everyone doesn't like 300 and 400 page books. I knew prosperity makes friends and adversity tries them, but damn I took it as if she was being cold to me. I guess it all got scrambled in my head because I'm THE PATERSON PIMP.

Well, as she walked away I called her a million bitches and hoe's in my mind. I remember even telling her that she reminded me of my *mother!* Enough said.

After that whenever we saw each other in passing the big hellos got smaller and smaller. I even lost the urge to massage her tonsils with my fat friend in between my legs.

July 27, 2008, was approaching...the day of my BOOK RELEASE PARTY! I invited her and the owner of the African Book store. They both came and showed support. I had comedians, rap groups, live band, free food and over 150 people attended. It was a night I'll never forget.

How a little boy born a Jehovah Witness turn PIMP could write a book *THE PATERSON PIMP* about his life and get so much support from family and friends and Paterson.

It was September 23, 2008, and I was set to do a Book Discussion at the Paterson Free Public Library. When I stopped by to speak with my man who works there and who had made it all possible. He asked me did I have a problem with *Anonymous*. He said he had mentioned my Book Discussion to her and she frowned and made a sucking teeth gesture. Wow! Did she really, really have a problem with me? I was flabbergasted.

Then one day just like "SYBIL" with a million personalities she began to talk to me and even told me about the Harlem Book Festival for 2008. I attended and spotted her there, sitting at her table selling her book *Anonymous* with a friend of hers I knew him from my younger days. She was most definitely making moves. But something I noticed about the guy she was with. I had met him many years ago on 17th Ave. He was a well-dressed hustler, a little older than me. I always liked his style even today. When I found out that they were dating I felt like I knew the kind of man that turned her on. I felt if I ever got the chance I would use that to my advantage.

Well, a year has gone by and we are now back to the big hellos and positive conversation. We often run into each other at the African Book store. And this day, we were discussing her latest book, which was her 5th book, *Barracuda Bytch*. I suggested that "we" should collaborate on a book together. She wasn't quite sold on the idea, but I was optimistic and persistent in telling her that the collaboration would be a good idea, especially us being from Paterson. I mean lately we've been able to agree to disagree on numerous topics—from PIMPING to being an INDEPENDENT WOMAN. And I guess that's how we got here...

The idea is to write a book on different topics, different points-of-view...you know, real talk.

In this book, we'll give the do's and don'ts through the eyes and mind and from the heart on how we truly see and feel about things.

For instance, I'll tell you things about the difference between a WOMAN and a BITCH. And maybe, she'll give you versions of PIMPS and HUSTLERS, and how to tell the difference between a GOODMAN from a BULLSHITTER. So sit back and chill and I hope you enjoy the RIVALS...REAL TALK: Coming soon: THE PATERSON PIMP VS. BARRACUDA BYTCH

128-Randy Jackson a.k.a Jashon

SHOUT OUTS TO ALL MY BROTHERS LOCKDOWN

DONALD WRIGHT

MONTE "FATHER FIZZ" WADE (cousin)

GARY "MUTA" NERO

GREGORY "DON JUAN" SHANNON

KEITH "KAHEEM" HILL (17th Ave)

NATHAN "NASHON" JONES (17th Ave)

JIMMY "JUSTICE" JOSEY (17th Ave)

MATTHEW "SHYSTIE" JACKSON (nephew)

DASHAWN MITCHELL

FRANK "BOOBIE" CULBREATH

DARNELL "D-NICE" FLEMING

MYRON "BELOVE" WILBERLY (17th Ave)

MICHAEL RITTER

ANTHONY HUSKEY

FREDERICK STONE

WILLIAM "COOLSHAWN" SERMAN (17th Ave)

RONNIE "FAHEEM" SMITH

JASON "BLACKFACE" ZIMMONS (17th Ave)

"AZ" (17th Ave)

"CHARLIE" (17th Ave)

And to all Brothers and Sistas Lockdown, Keep Ya Head Up!

FRIENDS

To those who have given me support, kind words, and encouragement about *The Paterson Pimp Part 1.*

SHEEMA NEWMAN

BARBARA MORRISON

KIM JONES

ANTWENETTE GRASTY

MARVA HINTON

WANDA RICKS

PATRICIA HAMRICK ANDERSON

LEATRAVELLE FLEMING

LATOYA BRUNSON

LENA HALL

DACIA WRIGHT

LEIGH LA'C WHITE

DENA RODGERS

WENDY SMOOT LEE

PENNY WILLIAMS

CHERYL LYNN HODGES

DONNA MCFARLAND

I couldn't possibly name everyone who gave me congrats on my first book, but I would like to say thank you all very much from the bottom of my heart.

Before I close this book I would like to send out a couple of special shout outs to:

CURTIS BOYD: Whom I met in April '87 in Ft. Leonard, MO (ARMY). When I got to the barracks everyone was talking about how bad this guy was from East Orange, New Jersey. I went looking for him, not to challenge him or anything like that but I damn sure didn't want to hang with the weakest guy there. From that day on we've been friends, but more like brothers. With him down south and me still in Jersey, we hardly see each other. But you can bet we don't let too much time go by before one of us is calling the other to check up and make sure everything is ok with each other and our family.

SUPERFLAM: Who I had the pleasure of meeting a long time ago. Every time we meet it's nothing but a player's real welcome shared between two. If you ever met "FLAM" you would never forget him because he's always looking like the coolest player in the room sharp as a tack!

MACK BROWN: Mack and I go back to grade school. If you saw or talk to Mack you'll know he wasn't born to do anything but Mack!

ERIC "DARNEL" TAYLOR: We were rivals in the game back in the 90s when we both had the 2 Top Ho's in Paterson. "AVENUE D" always remember it's not how many times you get knock down, it's how many times you get up player!

And last, but not least a special shout out to 3 of my favorite critics:

ALICE S.
ANGIE F.
MARGIE J.

Keep drinking that haterade. When will people learn that any publicity good or bad is promotion for my books and me? Keep spreading the hate it only motivates me to work harder and do better.

When will people learn that emotional wounds hurt more and last longer than the physical wounds?

To be continued...

Coming Soon!

"FROM THUG 2 GANGSTER 2 GENTLEMAN
Spoken Word Album by Raking Dohunne

"MENTAL SEX"
Book of poems by Johnathan Belvin (my oldest son)

Sssss

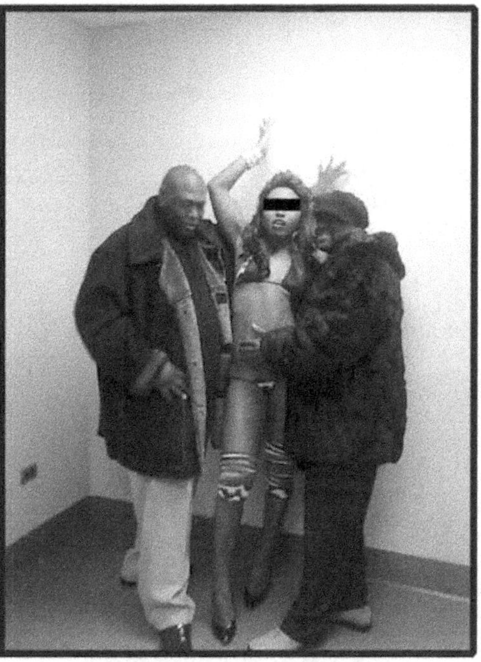

Playboy & Jashon "09"
X-Mas Party NYC

Jashon at Bachelor Party

Me & Ryan from Del State
(Knicks & Nets Game)

Just-I a.k.a Mikenice

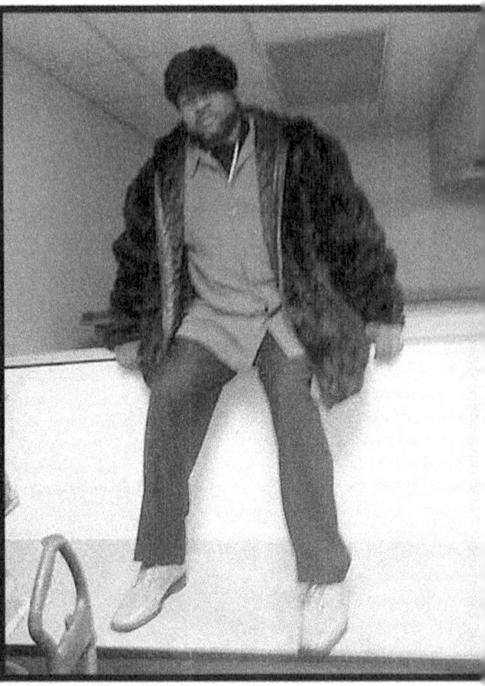

Jashon X-Mas Party

Jashon
-N-
Mitsubishi Baby

Fred Stone

Anthony Husky

Jashon -N- Yo-Yo

Jashon -N- IP

Jashon -N- Diamond

Black Jesus (R.C)
& His Lady
Summer Jam "09"

Jashon
Chillin

Jashon
-N-
Mitsubishi
Baby

17th Ave. Reunion

17th Ave. Reunion

Shadee(AH) in Green Hat Put Reunion Together

Playboy
-N-
Sex Appeal

Jashon
& I-Power (IP)
& Fire

"The Paterson PimP 2010".

Order Form

Photocopies of this form will be accepted for ordering

Book Title:	Price:	Copies:	Total:
My Soul Is Still Pimpin	$12.95	_____	_____
The Paterson Pimp	$14.95	_____	_____
Shipping & Handling			
Per Book	$4.95	_____	_____
For Inmates	$0.00		$0.00
		Total:	_____

NOTE: FREE S&H for all inmates who are currently incarcerated.

Accepted Forms of Payment: Check, Money Order, Online Payments via check or credit card through Paypal. If you are ordering for an inmate, please be sure to include their inmate number in the shipping address.

Shipping:

Name: _____ Inmate#: _____

Address: _____

City: _____ State: _____ Zip: _____

Send All Payments To:
J&M Production
507 Broadway, P.O. Box 133, Paterson, NJ 07514
Buy Online: www.ThePatersonPimp.com

www.ingramcontent.com/pod-product-compliance
Lightning Source LLC
Chambersburg PA
CBHW071703040426
42446CB00011B/1889